The
Granite
City

THE GRANITE CITY

A History of
Aberdeen

ROBERT SMITH

JOHN DONALD PUBLISHERS LTD
EDINBURGH

For
Jennifer and Graeme

ISBN 0 85976 483 4 (First Paperback Edition)

British Library Cataloguing in Publication Data.
A catalogue record for this book is available
from the British Library.

Typesetting and prepress origination by Brinnoven, Livingston.
Printed & bound in Great Britain by Bell & Bain Ltd, Glasgow.

Acknowledgements

A number of people helped in the making of this book. My thanks go to Aberdeen Central Library, who provided many historic photographs, and in particular to the staff of the Library's Local History Department, whose research assistance was invaluable; to Aberdeen Journals, for supplying a number of pictures; to Aberdeen Development and Tourist Department for colour pictures; and to Aberdeen Art Gallery for the cover picture.

I would also like to thank Edinburgh University Press for permission to use lines from George Bruce's poem, *Aberdeen, The Granite City;* to Leicester University Press for lines from *A Letter to Anne Ridler;* and to Buff Hardie and Steve Robertson for permission to reproduce 'Scotland the What' material.

Finally, a word of gratitude to my wife, Sheila, for her constant help and encouragement, and to others, unnamed, who, consciously or otherwise, fed me the information from which this book grew.

Robert Smith
Aberdeen

Contents

Introduction

The brown land behind, south and north
Dee and Don, and east the doubtful sea,
The town secured by folk that warsled
With water, earth and stone; quarrying,
Shaping, smoothing their unforgiving stone,
Engineering to make this sufficient city
That takes the salt air for its own.

from *Aberdeen, the Granite City,*
by George Bruce.

Aberdeen is reaching out to the challenges of the twenty-first century. With the coming of the year 2000 it can look back on two centuries of growth in which it has mushroomed from a town of ten crooked streets to a flourishing community of nearly 250,000 people. In the past thirty years it has floated to prosperity on a multi-billion pound bubble. It became the Houston of Europe, a town where the drawling accents of Texas mingled with the broad North-east Doric. Then it slipped confidently into the last decade of the twentieth century. Despite the oil boom, the city changed little in those early days, at least outwardly, but with the birth of a new century a new Aberdeen has also emerged. Bulldozers have blasted and gouged out the historic heart of the city, so that it has become a city of shopping malls, neat, neon-lit, and irrevocably soulless.

There is one thing that will never change. Aberdeen will remain the Granite City whatever happens, for nothing can blot out its native stone. The North-east writer John R. Allan once called it 'an unconquerable stone', but clearly didn't like it, partly because it could never lend itself to 'romantic twirly-wirlies', but mostly because it was too bright when the weather was fine and too grim when the weather was cold. I like to think of it as the poet Iain Crichton Smith saw it — 'a town of pure crystal'.

So, as we move into the new millenium, it is time to look at where the city has been and where it is going. This book examines the changes that have taken place. It turns the clock back to the days of whaling and sailing, to the time when Aberdeen clippers sailed the seas in the great 'tea races'. It strolls through

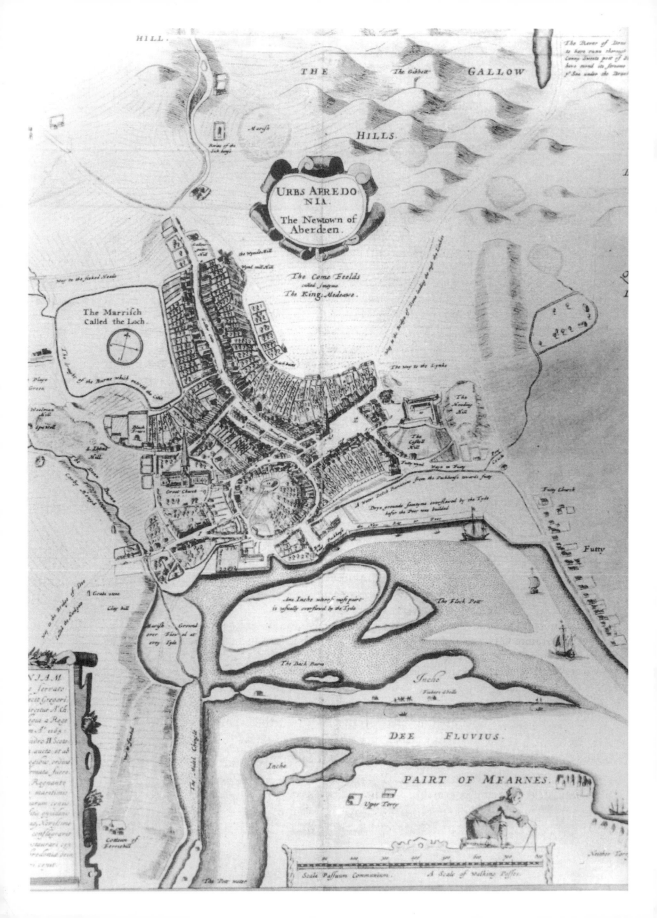

URBS ABREDONIA.
The Newtown of Aberdeen.

the past with some of our writers and artists, goes on parade with an Aberdeen in arms, and sits in on the deliberations of our City Fathers. From the seamy streets of the Lochlands to a gallows hill and a hill that vanished, the book sets out to show an Aberdeen unfamiliar to many of the people who live in it.

To put such a story into perspective, you have to visualise Aberdeen as it was two or three centuries ago — to see it as Parson James Gordon of Rothiemay saw it when he drew up his famous map of Aberdeen in 1661. He produced a bird's eye view of the city which won him an award from the Council of a silver cup, a silk hat, and 'ane silk gown for his bed-fellow'. It was said that the Parson was 'at great paines in draughting it upon ane meikle cart, which he delivered to the council! weill done'. A 'cairt' or cart was the old Scots word for a map or a chart, and this 'meikle' one measured 30in, by 24in.

It is a fascinating piece of cartography. The map itself, and an inset map showing 'the nearest places adjacent about it', underlines how small a community Aberdeen was in the seventeenth century. There is an index with names like the Shipp raw Streete, the Musick Scoole, the Huckster Wynde and Marishall Colledge at the Grey freer kirk. In the inset map, places like Rubeslaw and Heazleheid are seen in hilly country well to the west of the town. Foresterhill is Froster Hill.

'The Way to the Stoked Heide' is also marked. Today, the way to the Stocket 'heid' is up the long, steep brae of Mid Stocket Road. There were three Stocket roads at one time - the Low Stocket, the Mid Stocket and the South Stocket, but there is nothing to show their significance in the city's history. This was once the old Stocket Forest, one of the seven Royal hunting forests of Aberdeenshire, granted to the city by Robert the Bruce in 1313 for services rendered.

This section of the famous map drawn by Parson James Gordon of Rothiemay in 1661 shows how the Granite City was laid out three centuries ago. The map included Old Aberdeen, but the part shown above concentrates on 'the Newtown of Aberdeen'. One of the most prominent features is 'The Marrisch called the Loch', the stretch of water (Gordon called it 'a puddle') which gave the name Lochlands to the Loch Street/George Street area, which is now the site of the Bon-Accord Centre. To the north a gibbet rises above a peak in the Gallow Hills, while to the left of the map is the 'gate' or road that led to the gallows - the Gallowgate. Another place of execution can be seen on the right — Heading Hill, east of the 'Castell Hill' — while Futty Wynd runs down from the Castlegate. There was no Union Street in 1661, and to build the Granite City's main thoroughfare the city council had to cut off the top of St Catherine's Hill. The hill, which dominates Gordon's map, is seen rising like a miniature Vesuvius above the harbour area and the Inches. Other landmarks to be picked out are 'the Great Church' — St Nicholas Kirk - Woolmanhill, Windmill or Wyndmill Hill near the Gallowgate, the 'Cottoun of Ferriehill', and the 'way to the stoked Heade', which Aberdonians know better today as Mid Stocket Road.

The forest, of course, has long since disappeared. Houses sprawl beyond the Stocket 'heid' through Summerhill and Mastrick, following the pointing finger of the Lang Stracht along the old Skene road to the suburban neatness of Westhill. It took a long time to get this far. Towards the end of the eighteenth century the city was creeping out towards Loanhead, near which was the common pasture of the town. The Stocket slopes were under cultivation, but farther out to the west and south-west there was nothing but wild moorland. Earlier that century, the Stocket was 'a dreary waste, in which scarcely anything was produced except furze, broom and detached pieces of heath'. There was also an abundance of 'bogs and spouty marshes'.

Most of this wasteland belonged to the Corporation, who turned their attention to it after the 1745 Jacobite Rising. In 1750, a large area of the Stocket was planted with Scots firs. It is more than likely that the tiny strip of woodland still to be seen at Oakbank is all that is left of it.

Up until the last war, the Stocket brae was a favourite Sunday walk with people living in the area. Beyond St Ninian's Church you were 'into the country'. At the top of the Stocket brae, where the frenetic traffic of Anderson Drive now rushes east and west, you could look across the distant rooftops to the sea, and when dusk settled over the town you came down the brae, out of the darkness, into the stained yellow light of gas lamps. Those were the days of the 'leeries', prodding the city into light with their long poles, pestered by small boys who, when they weren't puffing peas at them, chanted 'Leerie, leerie, licht the lamps, lang legs and crookit shanks'.

Change came slowly between the seventeenth and eighteenth centuries, for a plan produced by G. and W. Paterson in 1746 shows little difference from Parson Gordon's plan of 1661. At Sandilands, where the Gasworks were eventually built, the smells were less odorous in 1746. 'Here grow all sort of pot-herbs,' said the map. Pot-herbs also flourished in the Ferryhill area, which had good soil for turnips, parsnips and carrots, 'which ye inhabitants daily use'.

There was also a large bog at Ferryhill where people from the town dug for peats. A series of hills is marked on Paterson's map between the Stocket Head and Rubislaw Den. The entry on the map reads: 'These Mountains abound with great Heaps of Small Stones, collected together in different places, for what purpose is uncertain'. It was at that time, in 1740, that Rubislaw Quarry was opened, so that 'the Heaps of Small Stones' were probably from the first quarrying operations. The city of the future was being cut out of Rubislaw Hill.

The nineteenth century was a period of great change. The city began to stretch itself, moving away from the small huddle of streets around the Castlegate. It was a century that saw the making of Union Street and King Street, the coming of gas, the building of the Music Hall, the opening of new public parks and a new library, and much else. It was also a century that gave birth to men like the architect Archibald Simpson, artists James Giles, James

Cassie and John Phillip, and writers of the calibre of Joseph Robertson and John Hill Burton.

Today, eyes are fixed on new horizons. In the last decade of the twentieth century the emphasis was on the development of the city's economic base, and on such things as oil and fishing, education and research, industry, tourism and transport, and the city centre.

There has been a good deal of concern over what has happened in the city centre, mauled and bruised by modern shopping developments. Much of what has happened in the central area gives point to the warning by historian Fenton Wyness that by the time the eighties came around the city would have fallen from architectural grace. That was said more than twentyfive years ago and the fears that he expressed then are being echoed as we move into the twenty-first century.

Change, of course, always brings doubt. Back in 1870, a writer called William Buchanan wrote an intriguing little book called *Glimpses of Olden Days in Aberdeen*. He was worried about how the developers were tearing the city apart, and what he said then is no less relevant today. 'I don't know if they are as fond of changes in other places as they are in Aberdeen,' he wrote, 'but here they think nothing of demolishing factories for the making of streets and markets and raising of hotels on sites of former industries, such as is going on now in Market Street and Stirling Street, where they are raising a grand hotel on the site of a once-busy tan-work and cotton factory. Then we go turning churches and chapels into music halls, merchants' shops and workshops for mechanics; manses into public-houses, and letting off churches for building purposes.'

Houses were also being demolished in the name of progress. Buchanan said jokingly, 'It is a high time we had a bridge to Torry to let us out of this, for they will be taking our houses down about our ears'. The bridge is there now (it was opened in 1881), but the problems haven't changed. In 1870, improvement work was being carried out at the harbour and Buchanan foresaw bigger ships discharging their cargoes at the docks. 'More room will be wanted,' he said, 'and where shall we get it? Over the water, surely.' More than a century later, he would have been amazed, not only at the huge oil ships crowding the quays in Old Torry, but at the developments that have taken place 'over the water'.

We looked back on the twentieth century as the dawning of the oil age, but when the nineteenth century ended, our forefathers looked back on it as the age of steam and electricity. 'No period of the world's history has been so marked by progress as the last sixty or seventy years,' wrote the Aberdeen historian William Robbie. He wondered if his generation had reached the limit of human invention and if people who would be alive seventy or eighty years later would look upon nineteenth-century achievements as 'slow and antiquated'. He made one prediction. 'It is impossible to say what the future may have in store,' he said, 'but we feel confident that in whatever progress may be made by the country at large, Aberdeen will not lag behind.'

Aberdeen has certainly not lagged behind, and is not likely to in the next century. Whatever lies ahead for the Granite City, and despite its dreich weather, its cold stone, its occasional canniness and its reluctance to talk well of itself, it will still be a good place to live in. As for the folk who work out their lives in it, an assessment of them can be left to the great Circuit judge Lord Cockburn, who was well-known for his blunt, unsparing comments on people and places throughout Scotland. He bit his tongue long enough to say that Aberdonians were 'a kindly, hospitable, unceremonious, happy people'. It is a judgement that still stands.

CHAPTER ONE

Castle on a Hill

When Edward I, the Hammer of the Scots, came to Aberdeen in 1296, he saw 'a faire castell and a good towne'. Seven centuries later, he would have found an eighteen-storey block of flats on the site of the castle. No-one could regard this great slab of granite and concrete on Castlehill as 'fair', yet there are two schools of thought about the building, even among architects. On the one hand, it has been argued that it contributes positively to the 'scenographic ending of Union Street', while on the other it has been dismissed as 'mediocre' and 'unfitting in such an important setting'. There are actually two blocks of flats, the main one being Marischal Court, the smaller, half the size, Virginia Court. The city already has a Marischal Street and a Marischal College, and it is a pity that the name has been repeated here. It would have been better to call it Castlehill Court.

This historic site was once the hub of the city. It was from here that Aberdeen grew and prospered. Now its name has been virtually wiped out, so that only an insignificant street sign is left to remind us of the time when there was a 'faire castell' on the hill. Before the 'skyscraper' block was built, a military barracks stood on the site, but its dormitories were turned into tenement housing in the years before the war and the building ended its days as a slum. The barracks were demolished in 1965, but the dank, unhappy memory of them lingered on, which was probably why the city council shied away from using the name 'Castlehill' for the flats that rose in their place.

On the whole, the tenants of Marischal Court are blissfully unaware that they are sitting on a thousand years of history. The historian G.M. Fraser once said that the teachers of Aberdeen should take their classes to the Castle Hill and give them a history lesson on the spot. I doubt if any of them do, although things might have been different at the turn of the century when Fraser made the suggestion. There were no multi-storey flats then, and it is hard to see how anyone could be touched by a sense of history in today's setting, except, perhaps, on the roof of the building, where you have a different perspective.

Up there, looking down on the wide, grey sweep of the city, I thought of how Parson James Gordon had meticulously sketched out *his* bird's-eye view of Aberdeen, drawing on imagination as well as skill. It was a different view from the one that can be seen today. Instead of the oil-rich harbour and its crowded quaysides, Gordon saw the Inches, islands of sand and mud brought

Danny Breslin, former caretaker of Marischal Court seen on top of the eighteen-storey block of flats at Castlehill.

down by the Dee and often 'overflowed by the Tyde'. To the north was the Loch of the Canny Sweet Pots, which the River Don ran through before turning east by the Broad Hill to the sea. There were lochs, marshes and hills. King's College and Machar Kirk rose from 'the Old towne of Aberdone'.

The early mapmakers had a leaning towards bird's-eye views. One of them was Aberdeen's pioneer photographer George Washington Wilson, who was an artist before he exchanged his pen for a camera. His bird's-eye view of the city, published in 1850, provides a fascinating glimpse of mid-nineteenth century Aberdeen. He consulted maps and made countless sketches, many of them from high buildings. For all I know, he may have climbed to the top of Castlehill Barracks to take a look at the city.

So, with Parson Gordon and Washington Wilson at my elbow, I stood on the top of Marischal Court and took stock of both past and present. The Gallowgate, one of the earliest streets in the city, is shown on Gordon's map, as is the gibbet from which this old highway from the north took its name, but all you can see today in the Gallow Hills are kirk spires and skyscrapers and double-decker buses lumbering around the enormous circle of the Mount-hooly roundabout. The Spittal Hills are still there, but no one thinks of them as hills any more, and when you turn east to the sea the 'Qweens Lynkes' draw your eye down towards Futty, which they now call Fittie. Across the water, Torry was a handful of houses — Upper and Nether Torry — strung along the banks of the River Dee. They were, said Gordon, 'pairs of Mearnes'.

Washington Wilson's map seems to have been drawn from some invisible skyscraper over Torry. The harbour has taken shape. Sailing ships are berthed at the quays and a solitary steamer throws up smoke from its long funnel. Castlehill Barracks is clearly seen and George Street stretches north into the open countryside, while at its south end is the area where, 140 years later, they tore up the old town to make way for the Bon-Accord Centre. From where I stood on Marischal Court I could see Union Street cutting a swathe through the centre of the town, but on Wilson's map it runs horizontally across the plan. It would be difficult to fault his sketch of it.

Danny Breslin was my guide on this roof-top exploration. He was caretaker of Marischal Court, with 108 flats under his control, which meant that he had to look after the needs of more than 200 people. He had, he said, no friends, because in his job he couldn't afford to play favourites, but as he travelled up and down his 'skyscraper' domain, keys clanking at his waist, he was clearly as indispensable to the tenants as the lift which is their link with the outside world. Flowers and coloured carpets decorated the landings. Twenty-one years in the Gordon Highlanders taught him how to handle his job as majordomo of the modern Castlehill 'barracks'. He had been caretaker for six years when I saw him. Born in Glenkindie on Donside, he is fascinated by local history and was well aware that a large slice of it lay under his feet on Castle Hill.

He liked to tell the story of how Jamie Fleeman, the Laird o' Udny's fool, once visited Castlehill Barracks. The commanding officer of an English regi-ment stationed there claimed that his grenadiers were the best wrestlers in the country. Tired of his boasting, the Laird of Udny bet him twenty guineas that the lad who herded his cows could throw the strongest man in the regiment. When the contest took place, the weakest soldier was put forward. Jamie threw him without any bother. A second, more powerful soldier was also thrown to the ground. Finally, the strongest man in the regiment stepped forward. He met the same fate.

'Hiv I got to throw the lot?' asked Jamie. 'Can ye nae get them tae send in three at a time? — I'll be late hame for the nowt.'

I wondered what the Laird o' Udny's fool would have thought of Castlehill now. Danny counted off the landmarks in the way that Jamie Fleeman would have counted off his 'nowt'. Brimmond Hill lay in the distance, and the tall

The view from the roof of Marischal Court, with Justice Street immediately below and West North Street flanked by car parks. The three gable-ends to the left of West North Street are actually one building, the old Corporation Lodging House — the 'Model', home to hundreds of homeless people over the years. The 'Model' was closed and has now been turned into housing accommodation.

radio mast above North Anderson Drive. Between West North Street and King Street was the Safeway superstore, and here and there kirk spires poked their spiky fingers into the sky. There are over fifty church spires in Aberdeen, and a good many more that have nothing to do with the kirk, but Aberdeen's once-famous skyline has been polluted by high-rise flats. I was standing on one of the offenders.

Below us, on the north side of Marischal Court, we were looking down on a group of streets where picture palaces (or cinema fleapits, depending on your degree of tolerance) sprang into life early this century. One of them was Bert Gates' Star Picture Palace, the Starrie, which opened in Park Street in 1911. Those were the days when Bert and his wife Nellie stood behind the screen and knocked coconut shells together to create the sound of horses' hooves. Then there was the Casino in Wales Street, which stood on the site of a waste factory, formerly a slaughterhouse, and backed on to the Starrie, while the Globey in Nelson Street (nobody ever called it the Globe) ran 'penny matinees' on Wednesdays and Saturdays. The jokes flew thick and fast; it was said that if you went in wearing a shirt you came out with a 'jumper'. They were noisy and ill-lit and they probably earned their 'fleapit' reputation, but going to the pictures nowadays is a dull business compared to seventy or eighty years ago when you could enter a magic world for a few coppers or a jam jar.

All that has gone. Now the boulevard picks itself up from the Park Street roundabout and sweeps down past neat and tidy streets to the Beach Ballroom and the Prom, provoking memories of the days when open-air tramcars rattled towards the sea-front loaded with bucket-and-spade sun-worshippers. There were times when the golden sands were black with people. For years, planners dreamed of how they could bring back the crowds, but cold economics and a snell wind off the North Sea always seemed to cool their ardour. At long last, however, it looks as if the prize has been won, although it may not be to everybody's taste.

The planners looked ahead to the new Millenium and saw it as the Popcorn Age, with drivethrough burger bars, 'Cosmic' bowling lanes, and a salute to the New World with names like Frankie and Benny's New York Italian Restaurant and the Daytona Bar-Diner. 'They thankit Bruce for keepin' a' the English oot o' reach', sang Harry Gordon. 'Ye see it hidna struck us then to advertise the beach'. Well, it has struck them now' but even if the English never return to the Beach the home-grown customers are lapping up the razz-ma-tazz of Aberdeen's own Blackpool. The old days and ways are gone. Now there is an Amadeus night club, a multi-complex Virgin Cinema — with pop-corn! — and a lot more besides, all packaged inside a new Queen's Links Leisure Park. On the other side of the boulevard there is an ice-rink, a swimming pool and a new hotel called the Patio.

From the roof of Marischal Court, looking from the south side, you can see Virginia Street curving up from the harbour. Its name, like that of Sugarhouse Lane dates back to the middle of the eighteenth century, when sugar-refining began in Scotland, and Aberdeen had a thriving trade with the West Indies and America.

But it was another kind of trade I was thinking about when I stood watching the traffic in Virginia Street. It was in Water Lane, a narrow, cobbled alley off

The Mannie o' the Well looks up the Castlegate to the Salvation Army Citadel, or the 'Barracks', as it was once called The Citadel, built in 1896, replaced the 1789 Record Office, a two-storey Georgian building. The Justiciar's Court House stood on the Citadel site, then known as Castlesyde, in medieval times. The Citadel architect, James Souttar, chose Balmoral Castle as his inspiration for the Salvation Army building.

Virginia Street, that Thomas Hunter was born in 1867. The folk of Aberdeen knew him better by the name he was given in a piece of local doggerel:

> If ye want a knocker for yer door,
> Or a hoose tae fit yer floor,
> Ging tae Cocky Hunter's store
> In Aiberdeen.

Cocky Hunter was King of the second-hand furniture trade in Aberdeen, although he sold a lot more than furniture. It was no idle boast that you could find anything from a needle to an anchor in his store. He was once asked for half a loaf of bread and, not to be outdone, sold the loaf he had brought in for his daily 'piece'. He opened his first second-hand store in East North Street in 1903 and a second one in Commerce Street five years later. When there was a market in the Castlegate he would get up at four o'clock in the morning, load a handcart with goods, and push it to his stance. He died in 1925 and at his funeral crowds packed the streets from Commerce Street to Trinity Cemetery. The cemetery was kept open until dark so that hundreds of his friends could file past his grave.

His eldest son Alec inherited the title Cocky and became no less famous than his father. When Bert Gates brought in local allusions to brighten his shows at the Starrie, he often used Cocky the Second as the butt of his jokes. Alec opened up a second-hand store in South Mount Street, while his brother Bill took over the premises in Commerce Street. The floors of the huge South Mount Street building groaned under the weight of goods of all description — sideboards, chairs, grates, bikes, sewing machines, cat's whisker wirelesses, paintings and old phonographs. There was scarcely room to walk through this Aladdin's Cave; bikes and bedsteads spilled on to the pavements.

In 1937, the building and most of its contents were destroyed by fire, and today the site houses the Rosemount Square flats. Perhaps it was fated, for the Castlegate was the spiritual home of the Hunter family and in 1938 Alec took over the old Sick Children's Hospital in Castle Terrace. Cocky Hunter's remained there until 1972, when it was bought by a property company. Alec died in 1961. In 1975, Bill Hunter's premises in Commerce Street had to make way for the new inner ring road from Virginia Street along Commerce Street to East North Street. The advertisement in the *Evening Express* announced 'Cocky Hunter's Closing Down Sale'.

When I was with Danny Breslin he pointed out the roofless building in Castle Terrace where Cocky Hunter had once reigned supreme. Now it has gone and an imposing new housing development looks down on Virginia Street and the harbour. The broadcaster and poet George Bruce wrote a poem about the sounds and 'sea smells' of this area, where the trams came clattering up from the Beach. The iron tram, he wrote, 'said bad words when it hit the cassies in Constitution Street, swore and screamed at the granite barracks at Castle Hill'.

From where I stood, looking up the long, straight line of Union Street, I could see in front of me another granite barracks. At one time, the Citadel was known as the Salvation Army Barracks, and the 'soldiers' who lived there had sin and poverty to fight. The Citadel is the dividing line between the Aberdeen of today and a piece of its squalid past. On one side is modern Union Street, glittering with oil prosperity, while on the other side, the east side, just behind the Citadel, is the spot where a century ago a notorious alley called Sinclair's Close housed 'the rummiest characters Aberdeen ever produced'. It was said that there were more robberies committed in Sinclair's Close in a year than in all the other rookeries — meaning rowdy, disreputable places — in the city put together. William Thom, the Inverurie poet, lived there, but that was long before it had become a slum.

The old, the blind, the lame and the lazy made for Sinclair's Close. There

'If ye want a knocker for yer door, ging tae Cocky Hunter's store...' This was Cocky's furniture store in Castle Terrace, where you could get anything from a needle to an anchor. As can be seen from the picture, there wasn't enough room in this second-hand Aladdin's Cave for all the Hunter treasures. Bikes, beds, chairs and tables overflowed on to the pavement outside the building. Picture by courtesy of Aberdeen Journals.

they could get 'a guid strae shak'-doon' on the floor for a bawbee, and if they had begged enough money that day they could pay for a wooden-bottomed bedstead covered with old sacks, sewed together and stuffed with chaff. If they were unable to find a place in Sinclair's Close they usually ended up in the hands of an official known as the cleeker, who threw them in the workhouse until the bailie could hear their case and throw them out of the town.

Not far from the Citadel, in East North Street, is the place where the human flotsam and jetsam of the twentieth century came for a bed. I saw it from the top of Marischal Court, looking unfamiliar because from eighteen storeys up its three gable ends seemed to run together to give the four-storey building an immense depth. This was the Corporation Lodging House, better known as the Model or Modeller. Opened ninety years ago, it was called the Model because it was meant to be a model for the future, an example of how a civilised society should look after its down-and-outs.

There were no cleekers awaiting the unwary outside its doors, but towards the end of *this* century its earlier boast of an enlightened approach to human misery began to look as shabby as the building itself. From outside it looked grim and grey, and, inside, its lodgers slept in row upon row of 6ft by 4ft cubicles. Nearly 300 men were accommodated each night. In August, 1988, its doors were closed for good and its 'guests', some of whom had lived there for nearly half a century, were sent off to other hostels in the city. The building was gutted and restored as housing accomodation.

I came down from Danny's Kingdom and took my leave of him. He is retired now and when the new caretaker, Ian Findlay, took over, Danny went to live in another multi-storey flat at Denburn Court. I joked with his wife Freda about still enjoying 'high living', but she said, no, they were only on the seventh floor — and there are twenty-one storeys in the Denburn 'skyscraper'. Ian Findlay and his wife Ann had been at Marischal Court for six years. Before that they lived and worked in Ballater, but Ian got a job in Aberdeen and they decided to move into town. The chances of getting a house were remote, but Ann saw an advertisement for a caretaker for Marischal Court and applied. They got the job, and now live in a firstfloor flat in the multi-storey complex. The spartan-grey lift dropped me eighteen floors to the entrance hall of Marischal Court. I wondered what would have happened if, like some subterranean Jules Verne machine, it had continued its downward journey. I once heard that there was a secret tunnel under Castle Hill, but when I inquired about it I was told dismissively that it was probably the sewage system. Later, I came upon some correspondence that persuaded me it was not.

Back in 1893, writing in a publication called *Scottish Notes and Queries,* a William Horne described how, while making sanitary improvements to a warehouse in Castle Street, he came upon a concealed passage leading to Castle Hill. The opening was 5ft 6in high by 4ft 6in broad. The passage was wet and slippery, but one of his men crawled along it with 30 fathoms of rope attached to him. He covered about 50 yards until he was under the site of what was then the new Salvation Barracks, but his light began to flicker and he turned back. About 20 yards along the tunnel he found a sword thrust into the roof up to the hilt. Another letter-writer told of how, sixty years earlier, a party of men had gone up an underground passage running from near St Clement's Church.

There was also a letter from a correspondent in Australia, who said that in 1829–30, when he was a lad of ten or twelve, he and his mates had explored a passage which entered a little to the east of the point where Hanover Street joined Commerce Street and Castle Terrace. They carried a candle with them and reached what they thought was the centre of Castle Street. Here the passage turned right towards Marischal College, where 'dissection was carried on'. At that time the town was buzzing with news of the Burke and Hare

Three aspects of Castlegate history are brought together in this picture. There is the Mannie o' the Well, which stood in the Castlegate until removed in 1852. In 1972, the Mannie came back to the Castlegate to take his place on the restored Plainstanes. The old Plainstanes, dating back to 1760, was where merchants met to discuss business, talk politics, and exchange gossip. In the background is the Royal Athenaeum, best-known at one time as Jimmy Hay's restaurant. The Athenaeum was part of the Union Buildings, designed by Archibald Simpson. The whole building was burned out in 1973 and later rebuilt as office blocks.

murders in Edinburgh and the burning of a 'Burking House' in Aberdeen, and the boys, thinking they might end up as anatomical specimens, turned back.

From these and other accounts it seems as if Castle Hill is riddled with tunnels. When Sir Samuel Forbes of Foveran wrote his description of Aberdeenshire about 1715 he mentioned that there was nothing to be seen of Aberdeen's ancient castle 'but some subterraneous vaults'. In 1741, the city council employed tradesmen 'for making two vaulted places at the Castlehill, the one for holding the Powder belonging to the town, and the other for Powder belonging to the Military'. When another Castlegate close, Burnett's

Close, was demolished late last century a secret passage was discovered in a house belonging to a merchant, Robert Burnett, who gave the alley its name. It ran from the cellars of the house to the shore, which suggests that Mr Burnett had been engaged in some illicit trading.

Castle Hill looks little like a hill from the Castlegate. It is only when you see it from Virginia Street that you can imagine how it must have looked centuries ago. Parson Gordon said that the top of it was flat, not much higher than the street, and that 'the syde of it nearest the shore is verie steepe'. Part of a wall of the fort that Cromwell built can still be seen, but there is nothing left of ancient St Ninian's Chapel, which stood there until 1794. Strip off the layers of history and you go back to Bruce and Wallace's time. Wallace's forces are said to have attempted to recapture the castle from the English, and in the summer of 1308 it was taken by the citizens of Aberdeen for Robert the Bruce.

From the site of Cocky Hunter's store, Castle Terrace runs down the line of what was marked on Gordon's map as Futty Wynd. Part of it was at one time called Castle Brae, but last century it was better known as Hangman's Brae. Johnnie Milne, Aberdeen's last public executioner, lived in a house there. There are differing stories about Johnnie's background; one says that he was a farmer from Tillyskookie, at Corse, another that he was a dyker or labourer from Old Aberdeen. He was sentenced to seven years' transportation for stealing some beehives and got a pardon on condition that he accepted the hangman's job.

Round the corner in Commerce Street is Heading Hill, linked to Castlehill by an iron pedestrian bridge. The hospital for Castlehill Barracks was built there in 1799, but what took place on Heading Hill in the sixteenth and seventeenth centuries had nothing to do with healing. It is a peaceful place now, rising above the closed doors and shuttered windows of Commerce Street Public School, and the householders who live in the buildings on top of it have a pleasant view of the sea front, but it was here that one of the most appalling chapters in Aberdeen's history was written. The cold statistics from the burgh accounts of three or four hundred years ago tell the story:

Item, to Alex Reid, smythe, for twa pair of sheckills to the witches in the stepill	£1 12 0
Item, the 9th of March, 1596, for ane boll and a half of collis to burn the said witches	1 10
Item, for six tar barrellis	2 0
Item, for a staik, dressing and setting of it	0 16 8

Witch mania took hold like the plague in Aberdeen. In one year, twenty-three women and one man were burned for alleged witchcraft. In September, 1597, Dean of Guild William Dunn was congratulated by the council for the 'extara-

The historic Castlegate in the days when a Friday market was held in the shadow of the Mercat Cross. The recent attempt to revive it has so far met with little success. The early name of Castle Street was the Marketgate, showing that it was a market place as far back as the 14th century. Note the Duke of Gordon holding court in the centre of the picture, behind the Mercat Cross. The Duke's statue now stands in Golden Square. Picture by courtesy of Aberdeen Journals.

ordinarie panis' he took in 'the burning of the gryt numer of witches this yeir'. The reek of tar barrels and faggots was said to 'darken the air'. The more people were sent to the stake, the more it fed the ghoulish appetite of the public. The council had to pay for four spars 'to withstand the press of the people' when one woman, Margaret Clerk, was burned.

On the east side of Heading Hill the street sign says 'Castlehill' and no-one I spoke to had ever heard it called Heading Hill. So here again a little bit of history has been eradicated. Old maps show it as Heading Hill and the name should have been retained. Some names remain true to the past. Justice Street, for instance, stands as a reminder that the king's Justiciar 'kept his court beneath the sky on Heading Hill'. Other names have vanished, leaving tantalising questions about their origin. The land around Castle Hill was divided into 'crofts' or sections with names like Galcroft and Friars' Croft, but one had the curious name of Fill-the-Cap. There has never been any explanation of how it got such a name, but when Constitution Street was laid out there was reference to it being 'made out through the ground of Fill-the-Cap'.

There is something faintly ironic about the city council cramming its tenants into a multi-storey block on Castlehill. Four centuries ago they were trying to keep people off the hill. In those days, Aberdonians had no more respect for city regulations than they have today. For one thing, they were stealing the hill, carrying off loads of sand from it (the same thing was happening at Woolmanhill) and the council had to issue an edict threatening to banish such lawbreakers from the town.

Building without permission was frowned on then as it is now, and the penalty of being found out was the same — demolish the property. When Andrew Jack built a 'litill house' in 1578 he was told to take it down because it was 5ft inside the Castlehill bounds. A woman who had a gate put up at the back of her house was ordered to remove it because the right of entry from the rear of buildings to Castlehill had been denied to occupiers 'past memorie of man'.

It may be that the City Fathers of those days were trying to protect the environment. There was space around the hill, for Sir Samuel Forbes of Foveran noted 'two agreeable walks', one at the foot of the walls of the fort, the other 'higher and green on top of the terra'. From both walks there was 'a fair view of a large open field, cultivated like a garden and producing the best of herbs and roots'. There is still some open space between the Citadel and Marischal Court, so maybe the city council will bring back a touch of eighteenth-century elegance to the spot where Aberdeen's citizens took a Sunday walk on Castlehill.

The so-called scenographic ending of Union Street is dominated by the Salvation Army Citadel, built at the end of last century in the style of Balmoral Castle, with the result that the Castlegate is separated from Castle Hill in a way that it never was in earlier years. In Parson Gordon's time only a fringe of houses stood between the east end of Castle Street and the hill. Castle Street, or the Castlegate (the 'gait' or way to the castle), was once known as the Market-gate. It was the heart of the burgh, and it is only during this century that it has drifted away from its old, traditional role in the community. Cut off from Castlehill, it has become hemmed in to the north and west by traffic, so that the recently pedestrianised area and its flower boxes look totally alien.

When I stood on the roof of Marischal Court, I could see the red-striped awnings of the stalls at the Friday market. The idea of bringing back markets to the Castlegate is a nice tourist gimmick, but it is pointless to think that this is in some way packaging the past, returning the area to its former glory.

Nostalgia clings to the Castlegate like the 'sea smells' of George Bruce's poem, but the reality is different.

Most of the old Castlegate closes have gone, slum alleys like Sinclair's Close, the Cowgate and Mauchline Tower Court. Peacock's Close, where Aberdeen's famous dancing master, Francis Peacock, tripped the light fantastic, is still there, but a gloomy, uninviting alley it is. They should build a museum behind one of the Castlegate old closes, perhaps alongside the Peacock Printers, where there is a print museum almost on the spot where Edward Raban produced his first *Aberdeen Almanac*.

Here, Aberdonians could catch a flavour of the Castlegate's past. They could learn about the old Tolbooth, find out how criminals were hanged looking down Marischal Street, discover the Earl Marischal's Hall, which gave Marischal Court its name, and laugh at the antics of Feel Peter and Turkey Willie. They could even, if there was a restaurant there, sit down to a glorious meal of creamy Finnan haddocks and partan claws as their forbears did at the old Lemon Tree Inn more than a century ago.

CHAPTER TWO
The Lochlands

The ghost of Willy Godsman hangs over the Lochlands. Willy was a beggar who hawked and sang satirical ballads in the streets of Aberdeen early last century. He was as ugly as a satyr, with a hunched back, fish-like eyes, a turned-up nose and lame foot. Nevertheless, he had his brief moment of glory when he sold a broadsheet criticising the council's handling of the city's finances. The magistrates reacted by banning him from the Public Soup Kitchen. Deacon Alexander Robb, a local tailor, came to Willy's defence in a poem described as a 'sorrowful lamentation for the loss o' his broth'. His plea that this was harsh treatment for a first offence touched the bailies' hearts — Willy was allowed to sup his soup again.

Robb, who often tilted at authority through his verse, peppered it with lamentations and remonstrances. He scribbled a remonstrance when the Tolbooth clock stopped during an election and he dashed off a lamentation when the Mannie o' the Well was moved from the Castlegate to the Green. If he had been living today, it is almost certain that he would have penned a *Lamentation for the Loss of the Lochlands*.

The Lochlands is the old name for a part of the city where 270,000 sq.ft. of land was cleared to make way for the Bon-Accord Centre, a vast shopping complex that was the twentieth century's dying salute to consumerism. All during 1988, the noise of drills and bulldozers shattered the peace of the Loch Street area as buildings were demolished to make way for what has been called 'an exciting new shopping experience'. In 1989, the new centre, stretching between St Andrew's Street and Union Street, began to emerge from its concrete chrysalis.

Meanwhile, at the junction of Loch Street and George Street, a small, curiously old-fashioned building stood with its windows boarded up as if closing its eyes to the changes that were taking place across the street. It stood at the gable-end of the former Northern Co-operative store, whose ribbed and cantilevered architecture was universally detested by Aberdonians. The 'Co-opy' store was taken over by the John Lewis Partnership, who retained the old façade.

During work on the new John Lewis store a makeshift passage was made to allow pedestrian access to the building, which was for long the home of two organisations. One was the Bon-Accord Spiritualist Church, the other the Aberdeen Public Soup Kitchen, where Willy Godsman lost his broth.

The Soup Kitchen, which is now a restaurant retaining its name and its atmosphere of the old days, marks the end of the line for George Street, where tramcars once rattled down to St Nicholas Street and the terminus at Queen Victoria's statue. In a sense, it also marks the end of the George Street dream. As far back as 1790, when work began on the building of George Street, hopes were high for this new road to the north. 'From the spirit of improvement which so much prevails,' declared the *Aberdeen Journal,* 'there is little doubt but in a few years this will form a populous and elegant addition to Aberdeen.'

It may be that this workaday street had delusions of grandeur. Named after George III, its drab architecture is brightened by buildings with elaborate scrolls, finials and balconies. The Trustee Savings Bank building near Hutcheon Street was designed by the architect Dr William Kelly, who put the leopards — Kelly's Cats — on Union Bridge, but in George Street he settled for a solitary lion on a keystone above a Venetian window.

The truth is that George Street has never been an elegant street. It was always — or seemed to be — a street of tramcars and tenements. The trams came hurtling down from Kittybrewster, swayed and clattered past a windy corner called Split-the-Win', and lurched on past the Upperkirkgate to St Nicholas Street. It was a street where you went to the pictures at the City, or crossed the road to the Grandy (the Grand Central, which was anything but grand), and shopped at Isaac Benzies'. As for St Nicholas Street, stuck on to George Street like an untidy tail, it never aspired to be elegant, for it had 'Raggie' Morrison's and 'Woolies'.

There is something sadly ironic about what is happening to this corner of the town. The St Nicholas and Bon-Accord developments have blocked off one of the main thoroughfares from Union Street to the north, yet two centuries ago the idea of opening up such a route from the centre of the city was a bright dream in the minds of eighteenth-century planners. The first move came in 1754 when a Mrs Urquhart sold some tenements and yards to the Council to enable them to build a small street called Tannery Street from Schoolhill and Upperkirkgate to the Loch of Aberdeen. Later came George Street, in line with Tannery Street, and when Union Street was completed in 1805 the final piece of the jigsaw fell into place — the building of St Nicholas Street. This new street cut a way through from Union Street to Schoolhill, and

A picture that will stir memories for many Aberdeen folk...a convoy of trams moving down George Street to St Nicholas Street. This was a busy shopping centre long before the days of the malls. Here you had 'Raggie' Morrison's, Isaac Benzies, 'Woolies' and the 50/- Tailors. You met at 'the Queen' and went to the pictures at the 'Grandie'. Queen Victoria's statue marked the end of the line. The tramcars that came clattering down from Woodside and the Fountain passed each other on two 'loops' at St Nicholas Street before heading back up George Street. Now the Queen has gone — and the old shops with fuel. The great new route to the north from Union Street has been shut off by the St Nicholas and Bon-Accord Centres. Picture by courtesy of Aberdeen Journals.

from there the way was open through Tannery Street and George Street to the Inverurie turnpike. Finally, the name Tannery Street was dropped. Now, nearly two centuries later, St Nicholas Street has been choked out of existence by the St Nicholas Centre, and part of George Street — the old Tanneries — has been wiped out by the Bon-Accord Centre. So much for progress.

Pedestrians, of course, are able to walk through the malls of both centres from St Nicholas Street to Loch Street, coming out almost opposite the Soup Kitchen. The kitchen, which was opened in St Mary's Chapel at the turn of the century, moved in 1827 to a tumbledown old smithy at the bottom of a squalid street called the Vennel, where the present premises now stand. There the down-and-outs were given a basic diet of a chopin (a quart) of barley broth and a large roll of wheaten bread for a penny. There must have been other items on the menu, for Deacon Robb wrote about Willy never wanting 'for broth, for pottage, brose or kail'. Over 77,000 meals were served up in the twenty-eight weeks in which the kitchen was open in 1827. Aberdonians gorging themselves in the Bon-Accord Centre's Food Court may think of Willy and his precious broth.

There were hungry clients on the Soup Kitchen's doorstep. The Vennel was one of the worst slums in Aberdeen — 'an abode of filth and wretchedness' was how one local periodical described it. It ran from the Gallowgate to the Lochside and was cleared away in 1842 to make way for St Paul's Street. Its removal was held up by a lady called Mrs Wilson, who owned two houses in the Vennel and refused to sell them to the council at a reasonable price. They could never have foreseen that St Paul Street itself would one day disappear, vanishing under concrete.

It is difficult to believe that there was once a loch on these urban acres, yet three or four centuries ago it played a vital role in the life of Aberdeen. In Parson Gordon's day it fed three of the city's mills, yet it was an insignificant stretch of water — a 'pudle', Gordon called it — for by that time much of it had become marshland. Despite the shrinking of the loch, the 'fenny' (dirty) marshland around it was still known as 'the Loch'. Gordon's map shows it as 'the Marrisch called the Loch', and it is clear that the original loch covered a considerable area of land. The loch was irregularly shaped and its boundaries today would be, roughly, Hutcheon Street, Maberley Street, Spring Garden, Loch Street, Crooked Lane, St Andrew Street and Blackfriars Street.

The loch was fed by burns flowing from the north and west, including the Westburn and Spital burns. In 1507, a century and a half before Gordon produced his bird's-eye view of the city, the litsters (dyers) were ordered to wash and 'wauk' (beat) their cloths in a burn running from the west side of the loch. At that time, too, the council set out to clean the loch, ordering the inhabitants of each 'fire house' (a house with a chimney) to send a servant along to help with the work. The same order was repeated twenty years later.

The neo-Gothic façade of Marischal College has had its critics as well as its admirers. The college was founded in 1593, the original buildings being grouped around a courtyard at the rear of Broad Street. In 1837, Archibald Simpson designed a new quadrangle, with a gateway leading into Broad Street, which was lined with houses running towards the Gallowgate. At the end of last century, when major extensions took place, the Mitchell Tower and Mitchell Hall were added and the present Marischal College frontage was built. The architect was A. Marshall Mackenzie.

In 1603, the council decided that the Lochlands should be let out for the growing of grass. It was made clear that when the grass was 'roupit' (auctioned), anyone who unlawfully cut it or let 'kye' or horses graze on it would be fined 'fourtie schillingis'. There were complaints that 'geiss' (geese) belonging to townspeople were feeding on the grass and destroying it. There were also complaints that the city's water supply from the loch was being polluted by litsters. In 1632, a minute of the Town Council reported that the loch was 'filthillie defyillit and corruptit, not onlie be gutteris daylie rynning in the burne, but also be listeris and the washing of clothes'.

In addition, there were 'other sorts of uncleanness' which the council was too discreet to specify, but they included dumping slops and the contents of chamber pots into the Loch. Servant girls found guilty of doing this were ordered to be 'joggit for two hours'. 'Jougs' were pillories in which the victim's neck was enclosed in an iron collar. The result of all this pollution was that the council decided to bring pure spring water into the town through fountains or wells.

By the end of the eighteenth century the loch covered little more than the ground now occupied by Loch Street, and in 1790 a report on the Lochlands in the *Aberdeen Journal* provided a glimpse of what lay ahead. 'The population and extent of this place seems to be going on with increased speed,' it said. 'The well-known field called Lochlands, on the west side of the Gallowgate, is now partly feued out for building. It is to contain four principal streets — George Street, Charlotte Street, St Andrew Street and John Street.' By 1838, the Loch had completely disappeared.

There are few reminders of the old Lochlands in the Loch Street area today. The close at No. 44 Upperkirkgate, now nameless, was once known as Burn Court, and the burn it took its name from was the stream carrying water from the Loch of Aberdeen into the town through the Loch E'e or Loch Eye. It passed southward to the east of Tannery Street, supplying water for the pits of the tanyard, through Burn Court, crossed the Upperkirkgate under cover to Lamond's Court at No. 49 Upperkirkgate, where the St Nicholas Centre now stands, and ran behind St Nicholas Street to provide water for a water-driven flour mill. The flour mill was demolished about 1865, but the name Flourmill Lane still remains.

The Lochside Bar in Loch Street marks the actual site of the Loch. The present bar was built in 1955, but the original Lochside Bar came into being in 1908 and was demolished in a bombing raid in 1941. This local pub is the spiritual successor to a hostelry that stood in the Taproom Close, a street running between the Gallowgate and Lochside. William Thom, the Inverurie poet, who was born in the notorious Sinclair's Close, off Justice Street, must have known the Loch of Aberdeen well, for his mother moved from Sinclair's Close to the Taproom Close. At that time there was only a very narrow footpath at the side of the Loch, with wooden footbridges at Spring Garden, St Andrew Street and the Loch E'e.

The Gallowgate sits brooding above the Lochlands. This ancient street — the road to the gallows — was the earliest in the city. It lies to the west of the highest ridge on the hill, while Porthill Court, a multi-storey block of flats, marks the site of the port or gate which guarded the entrance to the town. Porthill was also known as the Windmill Hill. There was a windmill there in the seventeenth century and Gordon's map shows it standing on the 'Wynd mill Hill'. The Gallow Hills, with the gibbet that gave the street its name, are to the east.

The houses on the Gallowgate, whose gardens ran down to the Loch in

Aberdeen's first 'mall' — the now-vanished 'Co-opy' Arcade in Loch Street. Inside it, the Northern Co-operative Society had grocery, bakery, butchery and footwear departments, with a carpet, lino and hardware department upstairs. The shoe department had 1000 pairs of shoes in stock. Busy every day, the Arcade was sardine-packed at weekends. There was an elaborate granite fountain at one end of it. Picture by courtesy of Aberdeen Journals.

Gordon's time, were occupied by the town's wealthier citizens, but by the nineteenth century it had become a breeding ground for poverty and squalor. In 1876, during the trial of a man from the Gallowgate, it was recorded that his wife and six children were crowded into an attic measuring 11ft by 9ft. Nevertheless, it was a street that bustled with life. It had more old worthies and eccentrics than any other street in town, and it had characters like Betsy Belle, whose song was still being sung in the years before the last war:

The Gallowgate, the mediaeval route to the gibbet...a dingy, cobbled street which some people said could have matched Edinburgh's High Street had it been saved. The city's top people lived there, but as Aberdeen extended westwards it became a squalid street of overcrowded slum buildings. Now, on Porthill, multi-storey flats have taken the place of the tenements seen in the picture above. Picture by courtesy of Aberdeen City Libraries.

> Oh, my name is Betsy Belle,
> In the Gallowgate I dwell,
> I suppose ye'll winder fit I'm deein noo;
> Weel, I'm lookin' for a lad,
> Be he good or be he bad,
> Onything in breeks will dae me noo.

There was another 'Bell' who, a few years ago, teetered on the edge of a measure of immortality when her name was put forward for one of the yellow plaques which the city council has been putting up to commemorate its famous sons and daughters. Her name was 'Candy' Bell and she ran a sweetie shoppie in Loch Street, where youngsters drooled over owls' eye eggs, peardrops and cupid whispers. In the list of nominations drawn up for the council her profession was given as 'Philanthropic Shopkeeper', and if justice had been done she would have taken her place alongside such worthies as John Barbour and Francis Peacock in the Castlegate. So far, however, 'Candy' has been ignored by the city fathers.

Then there was 'Pizzie' Grant, who lived in Rhind's Court in the Gallowgate. James was his proper name, but everybody called him 'Pizzie'. He was barely 4ft 6in in height, smoked a cutty pipe about 1 1/2in long, and dressed in a dark, velvet coat, a muffler, and pantaloons six sizes too big for him. He worked occasionally as a coal-heaver, but mostly he lived off the coppers that people gave him. He was immensely popular and when he died in 1870 a local poet called James Ogg wrote:

> There's mony will miss him, we'll
>   a' feel a want,
> The toon's incomplete since we
>   lost Pizzie Grant,
> Cauld, cauld are their hearts — oh!
>   they're nae men ava,
> Wha think nae on Pizzie
>   since Pizzie's awa'.

This old highway to the north had something of the character of Edinburgh's Royal Mile, and, in fact, a former Principal of Aberdeen University, Sir William D. Geddes, said more than a century ago that the Gallowgate could be made as romantic and picturesque as Auld Reekie's High Street. Even in those days, however, progress and development was more important than preserving the city's heritage, and Sir William's dream turned to ashes. One of the victims of late nineteenth-century change was the building known as Mar's Castle, a fifteenth-century house said to be the town lodging of the Earl of Mar. It sat at the top of the Gallowgate brae and was described in 1894 as 'the only picturesque structure in the whole length of that dreary and dismal thoroughfare'.

Picturesque or not, Mar's Castle was doomed, for in 1897 the town council decided to demolish it as part of a scheme to improve the neighbourhood. Its removal, they said, would improve the amenity. Over the wall from the castle was the meeting-house of the Society of Friends, and 'the yard wherein the people called Quakers' buried their dead. This old house, with its grim memories of the persecution of the Quakers in Aberdeen, met the same fate.

If it was ever intended to preserve the Gallowgate, the opportunity has long since been lost. There is virtually nothing left that has any historical significance. At one end there is the Aberdeen Technical College, its glassy frontage winking across the road to Porthill Court, which is neither better nor worse than any other 'skyscraper' block in the city, while nearer to Broad Street is Greyfriars House, where the Granite City's tax returns come under scrutiny.

It doesn't look much like a castle, but this building in the Gallowgate was known as Mar's Castle. It is thought to have been the townhouse of the Earls of Mar during the 17th century. There was a great similarity between Mar's Castle and Provost Ross's House in the Shiprow. The 'castle', which lost much of its character when it was repaired in 1836, was demolished during street developments in 1897. Picture by courtesy of Aberdeen City Libraries.

'A congeries of harled concrete boxes' was how the writer Alex Keith described the street.

Nor is there anything left to tell us about the people who lived in the warren of courts and closes in the Gallowgate; Mr Watt and Mr Dingwall, for instance, who gave their names to Watt's Court and Dingwall's Court, or the folk who lived in Poor's Hospital Court and Plasterers' Court, or 'Pizzie' Grant, nodding 'Good morning!' to his landlord, Mr Macaldowie, the brushmaker, as he came out of his dilapidated property in Rhind's Court, not far from St Paul Street. Two courts close to each other had the name Milne — Milne's Court and Provost Milne's Court — but whether they were named after the same man is unclear. Provost Milne, who was described by the Circuit judge Lord Cockburn as 'an excellent octogenarian Whig', lived in 'a queer, out of the way, capacious, old-fashioned house' at No. 65 Gallowgate. Lord Cockburn said that the Provost had 'a still more queer and old-fashioned wife'.

Now, as James Ogg said, 'Pizzie's awa',' as are all the other shadowy figures who lived out their lives behind these dark pends. There is still a Candlemaker's Court, also a Candle Close, conjuring up a name that was known, not only to generations of Aberdonians, but, as the *Aberdeen Daily Journal* once put it, to 'every household in the country'. The name was 'Soapy' Ogston. It can still be seen — Ogston and Tennant, Ltd — above the door of an office almost opposite Porthill Court; not far, in fact, from Candlemakers' Court. This unassuming little building was said to be 'the handsome new offices at 111 Gallowgate' of a company with a worldwide reputation for 'hard, soft, toilet and powdered soaps' — and candles of all description.

'Soapy' Ogston is as much a part of the Lochlands story as the loch itself. His grandfather started the business in the late eighteenth century and 'Soapy' (his real name was Alexander) joined the company as a teenager in 1855. He was still paying a daily visit to the Gallowgate offices when he was ninety years old. He died in 1926.

The Ogston empire had its roots in Loch Street. In the 1820s it had a candlemaker's business at 52 Loch Street, and, after operating as a tallow chandler, became a soap and candlemaker at 84 Loch Street in the 1850s. It amalgamated with the Glasgow firm of Charles Tennant in 1898 and the Gallowgate story picks up at the turn of the century. The business was taken over by Unilever after the last war.

Back in 1905, 'Soapy' Ogston's was virtually destroyed by what was said to be the worst fire the city had ever seen. GREAT FIRE IN ABERDEEN, proclaimed the headlines in the *Daily Journal*. CANDLE-MOULDING DEPARTMENT DESTROYED. EXCITING SCENES — FIREMEN INJURED. 'Many people seemed to think that the city had been suddenly overwhelmed by fire,' reported the *Journal*, 'and for a time there was an extraordinary panic. Women ran shrieking as they sought to get out of the

This towering block of flats in the Gallowgate is Porthill Court, which takes its name from the Port, or Gate, which formed an entrance to the city from the north. The site was also known as Windmill Hill. There was a Porthill Factory here in the mid-18th century, built for the manufacture of linen. It was demolished in 1960 to make way for residential development.

impenetrable smoke; mothers screamed for their children, who could not be seen in the terrible gloom of the choking atmosphere, and several were heard piteously exclaiming, "My God! whaur's my bairns?" '

Barrels of fat burst, setting off explosions 'like a big battery of artillery', and thousands of gallons of water and paraffin wax melted by the fire flowed down Loch Street. This river of wax was nearly a foot deep. Dean of Guild Alexander Lyon and two newspapermen found their retreat cut off and were faced with the unnerving prospect of having to wade knee-deep across the lava-like stream. They were able to grab some empty boxes and planks and, using them as 'stepping stones', made their escape. It was estimated that the fire cost Ogston's nearly £60,000, but, happily, they were fully covered by insurance.

The 'Co-opie' — the Northern Co-operative Society — was the near neighbour of 'Soapy' Ogston. Dick Simpson, who was publicity supervisor with

This building on the north side of Schoolhill was the town lodging of George Jamesone, Scotland's first portrait painter. It was the work of Andrew Jamesone, father of the painter. Jamesone, who was born in 1588, lived in the Schoolhill house from 1625 until his death in 1644. When it was demolished in 1886 during the widening of Schoolhill there were cries of 'Vandalism!' Picture by courtesy of Aberdeen City Libraries.

the Northern Co-operative Society until his retirement, had another connection with the soap-makers. His father was distantly related to the Ogstons (his name was Edwin Ogston Thomson Birnie Simpson), but the nearest Dick came to an association with the King of Soap was when he worked as a boy with the Co-op and handled the goods from Ogston's factory. The bars, he once recalled, were about 15in long — great cakes of plain, yellow soap.

Dick had records of the Co-op 'divis' of a century ago. In 1862 the dividend was one shilling and fourpence in the pound, and in 1938 it reached a spectacular three shillings and eightpence (19p) in the pound — the highest dividend ever paid. He also had a copy of a poem written by Charlie Fullerton, the furniture manager, as a vote of thanks to a meeting of the board of directors in December, 1951:

> The Northern's Board of Directors
> Are the guardians and protectors
> Of the interests and the brass
> Belonging to the Working Class.

Charlie, of course, was right, for the Northern Co-operative Company, as it was called then, was formed in 1861 by a group of working-class men, who opened their first shop at No. 45 Gallowgate. The amount of the 'divi' was a perpetual source of dispute among shareholders, who, wanting more, bayed for the blood of the directors at their annual general meeting. Anyone who remembers the glorious rows that arose at such meetings must wonder if the Working Class had complete confidence in the Board's ability to look after their brass.

Nevertheless, 'Divi Day' was a great day in Aberdeen's calendar, surpassing the Trades Week holiday, the Timmer Market, and even Hogmanay. It came twice a year, in May and November, each pay-out lasting for four days. Thousands of housewives converged on 54 Loch Street. The queues lined the street, the office stairs, through the long office and downstairs to the Arcade. Harold Miller, chief clerk and deputy chief executive before he retired in 1971, was the King Midas of Loch Street. Every Co-opie check he touched turned to gold. I remember him telling me casually, 'I suppose I paid out £2 million'. The individual 'divis' could run to as much as £100 or £200 — a small fortune in pre-war days. The housewives cashed their checks and went into the Arcade to spend their money on a new suit or a new pair of boots, and sweets for the kids.

The Co-opie Arcade, with its tiled walls and high glass ceiling, was well ahead of its time. Built in 1905, it housed the grocery, bakery, butchery and footwear shops, while up a small stair was the carpet and lino department. The furniture department was on the floor above, and the drapery department

The Wallace Tower in its setting at Tillydrone. The tower-house, originally known as Benholm's Lodging, was built in 1616 on the Netherkirkgate leading to St Nicholas Kirk. In 1963 it was taken clown and rebuilt at Tillydrone, above Seaton Park and the River Don. The first tenant after its move to Tillydrone was the Aberdeen historian Dr W. Douglas Simpson.

stretched from Loch Street to the Gallowgate. It was, in fact, Aberdeen's first mall, built long before modern planners dreamed up the modern shopping mall. It is a pity that the developers didn't modernise the interior of the old Arcade and keep the granite frontage. It is an interesting thought that, with a little foresight, the Co-opie Arcade could have arisen Phoenix-like as the new Lochlands shopping complex.

Norco House, with its controversial frontage facing George Street, replaced the Arcade. Later, the Co-operative Society built their superstore at Berryden. When the Bon-Accord Centre was planned, the Society was given the opportunity of moving into the new complex, but decided against it, opting for future development at Berryden. Now John Lewis is in Loch Street. A museum was planned for Berryden, a permanent reminder of how it all began in the days when a 'hurly', a two-wheeled push-cart, was the only transport system operated by the Co-opie, but nothing came of it.

So the Co-opie has gone, and 'Soapy' Ogston's has gone. Innes Street, where the soap-factory fire drama was played out early this century, has also vanished, as has a handful of other streets leading off the Gallowgate. Young Street, linking Gallowgate with Lochside, has disappeared. It was named after Provost William Young, of Sheddocksley, who owned ground near the Loch. The Windy Wynd, down by Spring Garden, has also gone. John Phillip, the Aberdeen painter, is said to have been born in Windy Wynd, where his father was a shoemaker, although some say he was born in Skene Square. There is a plaque to him in Skene Square, where he lived as a child.

Berry Lane has been wiped out, but it has re-appeared in a different form near the south end of the Gallowgate. Here, almost on the corner where the first Co-op shop was opened, a new link road called Berry Place has been built, sweeping down from the Gallowgate to Loch Street, following the line of the Bon-Accord Centre. On the north side of Berry Place, sixty-eight flats have been built, which would have brought an approving nod from Provost Milne, whose queer, old-fashioned house stood almost on the same site.

Whether the Bon-Accord Centre would have met with his approval is another matter. This £26 million complex changed the whole pattern of commercial life in the city centre. The centre has three major stores, including C & A and Boots, and forty-six shop units on two shopping levels. Inside the Leisure Centre there is a six-rink indoor bowling hall, two squash courts, a bar and a restaurant. Car parking space is provided for 1,200 vehicles.

Nearly two decades ago, the Aberdeen architect and historian Fenton Wyness spoke of the city falling from architectural grace. His predictions have largely come true. Whether or not the Lochlands development takes us farther down this road, turning the Aberdeen of Archibald Simpson into a city of glass and glitter, remains to be seen. There have been mixed emotions over the Bon-Accord project, but there was an uneasy feeling that too much was going too

If you had lived in 1889 when this picture was taken you could have walked through the archway on the left and landed up in Marischal College. This was Broad Street when Marischal College lay behind it. All these buildings from the Gallowgate to Queen Street were swept away at the beginning of the present century to make way for the present Marischal College facade. The building marked 'S. Byres, Wholesale Fruiterer' was built in 1776 as a waterhouse, acting as a reservoir for water brought from the springs of Gilcomston and Ferryhill. The town's fire engines were housed under the reservoir in the late 18th century. The waterhouse was demolished in 1903, but the big clock in the picture can still be seen ticking away at the City Hospital. Picture by courtesy of Aberdeen City Libraries.

easily. 'Fat hiv ye deen t' my ain native toun?' asked A.M. Davidson in a poem called 'Vandalism'. He catalogued some of the things that had vanished... Strawberry Bank, the old Wallace Tower, Ragg's Lane and the Guestrow. Some things, he knew, were better away, but he wondered what would be put in their place — 'a curn spunk boxes (a number of match-boxes) wi nae sowl, hert nor face', he forecast.

There is nothing new in the kind of 'vandalism' that Davidson pinpointed in his poem. The same word was used by Alex Keith in A *Thousand Years of Aberdeen,* when he mentioned the demolition in 1890 of what had been the town-lodging of Scotland's first portrait painter, George Jamesone. There are two plaques near Donald Court in Schoolhill indicating the site of Jamesone's house and studio. It seems an odd thing to have two plaques, almost as if there had been a left-over sense of guilt at having destroyed what was said to be one of the most beautiful private houses in Aberdeen.

The garden of Jamesone's tall, turreted house, which was built in 1586 by his father, Andrew Jamesone, a master-mason, reached right back to the Loch of Aberdeen. The death knell of the house was sounded when it was bought by Wordie and Co., the road haulage firm, whose name was a byword in Aberdeen for many years. There was a timeworn 'Knock, knock' joke about 'een a' Wordie's horses': Knock, knock! Who's there? Ena. Ena who? Een a' Wordie's horses! Wordies, who wanted to extend their Schoolhill premises, planned to demolish Jamesone's house, and during the outcry that followed a group of archaeologists tried unsuccessfully to buy it in order to save it. John Morgan, a prominent builder who was involved in such ventures as the laying out of Union Terrace and the building of the city's library, regarded the demolition of Jamesone's house as part of the 'ruthless and wholesale destruction of many old and time-honoured landmarks'. Today, Wordie and his horses are commmemorated by Wordie's Alehouse at No. 16 Schoolhill.

There has always been this conflict between those who want to hold on to the past and those who want it swept away in the name of progress. Morgan was concerned, not simply with the loss of many of the city's historic buildings, but with what took their place. Some of the new buildings, he said, were 'flaring monstrosities'. There were streets and roads where architecture, taste and skill were non-existent. What will be said a century from now about the Lochlands of the 1990s only time will tell. The one thing certain is that it is probably the biggest development Aberdeen has seen since the building of Union Street at the beginning of the nineteenth century.

CHAPTER THREE
Unconquerable Stone

Aberdeen was built on three hills. Two of them, Castle Hill and the Gallowhill, are well-known, but not many people know the third hill. Yet, if you turn away from the grumbling traffic on Union Street and into what must be the shortest street in the city, St Catherine's Wynd, you are walking on top of it. Or, at anyrate, on what remains of it, for when it stood in the way of progress nearly two hundred years ago the town council had its head chopped off.

St Catherine's Wynd lies between St Nicholas Street and Broad Street. It took its name from St Catherine's Hill, a steep, round, conical hill in the middle of what is now Union Street. Parson Gordon's map shows it rising up between the Netherkirkgate and the Shiprow like a miniature Vesuvius, circled by buildings, with trees and gardens on its slopes. Gordon said that when you stood on top of it you could see 'the firth and river of Dee, the villedge of Torrie, pairt of the sea coast, and the nearest hills and corne feilds which ly westward of the citie'. From it, about 1716, Sir Samuel Forbes of Foveran saw 'the amusing sight of the River Dee, and its beautiful bridge', although why he found it amusing remains a mystery.

The hill was named after a chapel that stood there in the thirteenth century. At one time there was a gun on its summit, and it may well have thundered out the time of day like the gun on the Castle Rock in Edinburgh. It was certainly used for funerals. When Provost Alexander Aberdein died in 1756, the *Aberdeen Journal* recorded — 'At one o'clock, the bells began to toll, and the minute-gun fired from St Catherine's Hill, which continued till five, when the corpse was lifted.'

The highest point of the hill would have been where the entrance to the Adelphi is today. From here, you can actually walk down St Catherine's Hill. Adelphi Court is a *cul-de-sac*, but at the far end there are steps, now closed off, going steeply down the side of a disused church to the Shiprow, while another route can be followed through a pend halfway along the court. This takes you out between Provost Ross's House and the ABC Cinema, which stands on the site of the old St Catherine's Hall, originally known as the Cafe Hall. In 1908 it became Aberdeen's first permanent cinema, the Gaiety.

St Catherine's Hill was known locally as 'the brae'. It cradled some dubious characters in its lap, among them a woman called Grace Finlay, who was

Aberdeen's famous Rubislaw Quarry as it was in pre-war years. In those days, coach parties stopped to gaze down into the awesome hole. It was nearly 500ft deep and 900ft by 750ft at the top. The scale of it is shown by the tiny figure of a man in the lower right of the picture. It produced granite for over two centuries. Picture by courtesy of Aberdeen Journals.

A striking aerial picture of the hole from which the Granite City got its name. Here, Rubislaw Quarry is seen in its present setting, surrounded by houses and offices, fenced in, and hidden from public view by a thick 'crown' of trees on its rim. It is estimated that six million tons of granite came from this dark hole, which now has 180ft of water at the bottom of it. Picture by courtesy of Aberdeen Journals.

known to be free with her sexual favours — and not too fussy about who received them. William Anderson, a well-known poet, told how, when the 'neebors were fast i' their beds', this hot-blooded widow got visits from Archibald Black, a glazier, who had 'a humph on his back':

> There was ane, Gracie Finlay, wha dwelt i' the brae,
> A braw wanton widow o' forty or sae,
> Weel to do i' the warl, an' hearty an' hale,
> Wha sells in a sly way baith brandy an' ale.

Up till the beginning of the nineteenth century, the west end of the Castlegate was closed in by a block of houses, with two narrow streets, Exchequer Row and the Narrow Wynd, running into Castle Street from St Catherine's Hill. Beyond that was the great dip of the Denburn Valley, a scattering of houses, and open space. The city was looking west, but St Catherine's Hill was a seemingly impenetrable barrier to the expansion which a growing population and the city's rapidly-increasing trade were demanding.

In 1780, a plan was put forward to link Castle Street and the Green by a new street running over the brow of St Catherine's Hill. The idea was to lower the hill to avoid the levels being too steep. It was the first attempt to shake off the shackles of the Castlegate and open up a new route to the west, and if it had gone ahead the pattern of traffic in the centre of Aberdeen would have been completely different today. Nothing, however, came of it.

The breakthrough came twenty years later, when the town council decided to open up the city by building two great new arterial roads running north and west from the Castlegate. One was King Street, the other Union Street. The building of Union Street meant cutting through the north shoulder of St Catherine's Hill and erecting a huge, single-arch bridge over the Denburn. It must have seemed like a planners' fantasy to the ordinary folk of Aberdeen, for it was a formidable feat of engineering, but it set the seal on a century of remarkable progress in Aberdeen. It was also the first step towards the making of the Granite City.

The halcyon years of Archibald Simpson and John Smith, the architects who created the Granite City, still lay ahead, and in the early days of Union Street's construction there was nothing to show that it was to become 'one of the finest streets in the Empire'. On the south side, where the line of the street was marked by a low brick wall, you peered into the Green. The roofs of many of the houses stuck up above the level of Union Street and a number of house-holders realised that the council had unwittingly provided them with a shortcut to the new thoroughfare. They laid wooden gangplanks between the attics of their houses and the brick wall and stepped on to Union Street.

Some of the householders, with the canny Aberdonian's instinct for making money, saw business opportunities in this rooftop lay-out. There were cabinet-makers, joiners and sawtrimmers in the Green and those who lived on the top-floor attics stuck advertising signboards against their chimney cans, publicising their services to passing pedestrians on Union Street. But there were draw-backs to 'high life' in the Green. Householders whose lums were lower than the level of Union Street were often pestered by youngsters chucking stones down their chimneys.

Today, stores like British Home Stores and Littlewoods have taken the place of the brick wall, with back-stairs leading down to the Green. They have no room for development to the south except by bridging the Green, which Littlewoods and the Trinity Centre did a number of years ago, turning the west corner of the Denburn, where it meets the Green, into a dingy, cluttered cavern under the Trinity car park. When other companies talked of doing the same thing there was a rumble of alarm among conservationists, who saw the old historic Green disappearing under a conglomeration of multiple stores.

The Green, where open-air markets have been held since the Middle Ages. The picture above was taken in 1903. The Green takes its name from the Gaelic *grianan* — a sunny spot. The New Market, demolished in 1971, can be seen in the background. Picture by courtesy of Aberdeen City Libraries.

With a dual carriageway planned for Denburn Road and the Green itself marked down for conservation, the 'multiples' took their expansion plans elsewhere. Two of them staked claims in the Bon-Accord Centre. Boots and C & A each got 55,000 sq. ft. of space in the Bon-Accord scheme when it opened in 1990. This move away from what has always been the city's main shopping area raised questions about the future of Union Street. The planners' theory was that there will always be a demand for property in Union Street, but that a different kind of shop would move in when the big stores moved out.

Property prices would be the deciding factor. They have always been high on Union Street. As far back as 1868, Sir Alexander Anderson, who was Lord

The Green at the turn of the century, when farm folk came to town to sell their butter and eggs, vegetables and flowers, at the Friday market. Fishwives walked from Cove and Skateraw, south of the city, to set up their stances at the railway end of the Green. Looking down on the scene was the Mannie in the Green, or the Mannie o' the Well, as he was known when he first appeared in the Castlegate in 1706. He was removed from the Castlegate in 1842 and erected in the Green in 1852. He returned to the Castlegate in October, 1972. Picture by courtesy of Aberdeen City Libraries.

Provost of Aberdeen for six years, said that the value of property in Union Street was 'becoming fabulous — there had been a rise of 33 per cent, since 1858'. Whatever happens to Union Street as a shopping centre, it is unlikely that it will lose its granite-faced dignity.

Archibald Simpson and John Smith placed their indelible stamp on it in the first half of the nineteenth century and it remains. Union Chambers, the first building in the town designed by Simpson, is above M'Combie's Court, which was named after a bailie who made snuff. The court runs through to the Netherkirkgate, where Carnegie Brae takes over and plunges into the Green by the dungeon-like vaults under Union Street and Market Street, roughly tracing the line of St Catherine's Hill.

The Granite City is a tenement town, and nothing illustrates it more than these tenement flats in Rosemount Viaduct. The ground-floor flats of these five and six-storey tenement blocks were let as shops. The tenements in the picture drop down to basement flats in the Denburn. The flats have been modernised, so that the old brick toilets — the 'stairheid lavies' — have been removed.

The work of Simpson and John Smith (Tudor Johnnie, the city's first official architect) paces the mile-long length of Union Street. Among the buildings they planned are Simpson's Union Buildings, better known to generations of Aberdonians as Jimmy Hay's or the Athenaeum; the old Queen's Cinema, which originally housed the Advocates Hall; the Music Hall; the North of Scotland Bank, now the Archibald Simpson Restaurant, and the Facade of St Nicholas Churchyard. This colonnade always strikes me as being something of a Folly, as if some great architectural project had been planned and had never got beyond the entrance stage. Smith was asked to provide a front to the churchyard and an entrance into it and this is the result. Curiously, it works, stylishly filling an area that would otherwise look like a missing tooth on the face of Union Street. Before the Facade went up, circuses and menageries used the ground.

Some buildings have gone; the Trinity Hall, for instance, designed by John

The glory days of the New Market are recalled by this picture of the main hall of the building designed by Archibald Simpson. The hall was 320ft long, while there were more shops in the gallery upstairs. The Market, which had an impressive entrance facade on Market Street, was burned out in 1882, but was rebuilt. It was demolished in 1971, when it was replaced by the present shopping centre, which is a pale and tawdry shadow of the original New Market. Picture by courtesy of Aberdeen Journals.

Smith and his son William, and Simpson's New Market — 'Ye've flittit oor Tarnty Ha',' mourned A.M. Davidson, in 'Vandalism', 'Rugged doon the New Market and muckt up the Green'. The Royal Northern Club, which was once known at Crimonmogate's House, was Smith's work. It was demolished in 1963. Davidson wondered what had happened to the Northern Club, 'wi its snod Coonty snobs'. It wasn't only 'coonty snobs' who paraded in the elegant west end of Union Street when this building was erected in 1842. As the city began to grow, the town gentry began to move west.

There were already a number of houses in Union Place, which was Aberdeen's Harley Street, where many of the city's doctors lived, and as Union Street crept out towards it others joined them. The name was abolished in

Although Aberdeen folk tend to take it for granted, one of the most striking features of Union Street's architecture is the Facade, designed by John Smith in 1830. It is made up of twelve Doric columns with an arched gateway in the middle. Behind the Facade is the Kirkyard of St Nicholas, where many of the city's noted citizens are buried. Before the Facade was built, the ground there was used by visiting circuses.

1890, but if the owners and residents had had their way Union Place would still be there. They objected to it being swallowed up by Union Street. Interestingly, it is the West End of Union Street, the old Union Place area, that the planners saw as a 'secondary' retailing location for quality and upmarket specialist goods, partly because the rents there would be cheaper.

After Union Bridge was built, streets like Golden Square, Diamond Street, and Chapel Street began to mushroom in the new West End, followed in the 1820s by Crown Street, Bon-Accord Square and Bon-Accord Crescent. Archibald Simpson built a house for himself and another for his brother (Nos. 13 and 15) in Bon-Accord Square and it is there that a plain granite block commemorates this master of design, the man who did more than anybody to shape the Granite City.

He died in East Craibstone Street, not far from what is arguably the finest building in Union Street. Simpson built his Assembly Rooms in 1822. A. M. Davidson's 'snod county snobs' would have been at home here, for it was built by a group of wealthy landowners as a town club where they could pass the time by dining and dancing, gaming and playing billiards. Later, the Music Hall was built on the site of what was the banqueting hall and it is as the Music Hall that it has served generations of Aberdonians.

In its time it has gone far beyond the sophisticated pleasures of the lairds who first used it. In the dying years of last century it ran 'electro-drama' slides and films, it staged the city's first cinematograph shows, it presented 'Madame Lloyd's Grand Musical and Scenic Company', it held exhibitions and concerts, and for a short but glorious spell in 1922 it actually became the Music Hall Cinema. The last time the Music Hall was used commercially for a cinema performance was in January, 1930, when Dolores Del Rio wowed them in a silent movie called *The Trail of '98*.

It now faces a new century with considerable confidence, and with a Royal patron who is ready to put her best foot forward. The statue of Queen Victoria in the entrance foyer stood originally in the main corridor. During the restoration it was discovered that Her Majesty's big toe was missing, and when attempts were made to take a cast from another statue it was found that on this one she wore a slipper. In the end, it was decided to take the cast from a real foot, and now a stand-in toe sticks out from under the Queen's robe. Only the sharpest eye would notice that it is slightly out of proportion. The fact is that the real big toe belongs to a foot that takes a size 10 shoe.

Queen Victoria's change of location in the Music Hall is one of a number of shifts that have been inflicted on her in Aberdeen. Two of her statues stood at the junction of St Nicholas Street and Union Street, which gave rise to the familiar phrase, 'Meet you at the Queen'. The first statue, suffering from over-exposure to Aberdeen's dreich weather, was taken into the Town House in 1888, and its successor, erected in 1893, was moved, appropriately enough, to Queen's Cross in 1964. When a new Park and Ride route was being discussed in 1997 there was a suggestion that the Queen would have to be moved once again.

There is a house at No. 50 Queen's Road, built in Victoria's time, which attracts a large amount of attention from passers-by. This was the home of John Morgan, the builder. If Simpson was the master of design, Morgan was the master of stone. He was responsible for such diverse projects as the new Marischal College, Aberdeen Fish Market, and the Caledonian Hotel (originally the Grand). He laid out many of the city's streets, among them Fountainhall Road, Forest Road, and Argyll Place and Crescent, where the houses are built of two-tone granite. He also built twenty houses in Queen's Road.

The statue of King Edward VII dominates the corner of Union Terrace and Union Street. The King ousted his father, Prince Albert, when he took his place at Union Bridge in 1914. The statue of the Prince Consort, by Baron Carlo Marochetti, which stood there until it was replaced by the granite and bronze statue of Edward, was heavily criticised when unveiled by Queen Victoria in 1863. Prince Albert was moved to Rosemount Viaduct, where he sits in the shadow of the mighty William Wallace.

Morgan rode to success on the back of the granite industry, yet, paradoxically, he was not a complete convert to the use of granite. Aberdeen's grey granite, he said, had a fine sparkle in the sunshine, but there was another side to the picture. 'In some lights,' he declared, 'the granite looks cold, hard, repellent and colourless.' The unconquerable stone, as J. R. Allan called it, has had its share of critics.

Even the granite statues have come under fire. The Circuit judge Lord Cockburn, who was never at a loss for a devastating phrase, disliked the Duke of Gordon's statue — the first granite statue in Scotland, now standing in Golden Square. 'This duke's visage,' he observed, 'looks as if it had been rubbed over with oatmeal.' He believed that granite was the wrong stone for sculpting the human figure, particularly when a sculptor's subject should be shown warts and all. If a man had freckles or pimples there was a problem. 'The freckled face, if the granite be grey, or the pimpled or blotched face, if it be red, are insuperable objections,' he said.

At the west end of Queen's Road, beyond Anderson Drive, lies the big hole — Rubislaw Quarry. I remember the days when you could walk to a small, ramshackle wooden platform on the edge of the quarry and look down into that vast chasm, seeing tiny figures moving toy-like on the floor of the quarry. The Lallans poet, Alastair Mackie, recalled this 'sma signal platform, wi its widen snoot stuck oot ower the whin-bushes' in an article called 'My Grandfather's Nieve'. His father used to stand there, 'wi his lugs cockit for the thin cry o "Heave" fae hyne ablow', when he would signal to the crane man to start hauling up another load of granite.

That granite, loaded on to a cart, came down the elegant length of Queen's Road, the carters stopping at 'Babbie' Law's shoppie near Holburn Junction for a drink to clear the granite dust from their throats. 'O the lang straucht o Queen's road!' wrote Mackie. This is how he saw it as he looked back to his childhood in the years between the wars:

> The granite grandery o thon road I traikit as a loun wi the faimily. Hou we ferlied at aa the grand hooses on ilkie side aa the wey up! They keekit atween the green bells o trees that the blackies jowed; the crook o their graivel paths as they swung their flooers and bushes to the front door; or their trig rockeries and gressy swatches o lawn crawsteppit up to the windas; their privet hedgeraws burst thro the jile bars of their black railings, and the trees, fu o themsels, blockit oot the facades or owerhung the pavements as we lytert aneth their huggert pends. I used to think; the deid hooses of the livin. Or was't, the livin hooses o the deid? Naebody was ever at the windaes, naebody on the lawns, naebody we ever kent bade in them. 'Fishmerchants' hooses' my father said. Or the quarrymaisters? Fa ained the quarries? I never heard tell.

Alastair Mackie, who was a teacher in Anstruther, came from a granite family — 'I cam oot o a granite quarry-hole'. His grandfather, father and uncle all worked at Rubislaw Quarry. They lived in Rubislaw Park Road, which is a good deal different today from what it was a century ago. In 'My Grandfather's Nieve', which he wrote in 1975, he vividly described their quarryman's home; the 'foosty stink o the room wi the lie-ins', the 'nippet' living-rooms, the sewing machine, the press below the sink where the pots were kept among the 'craal o spiders', and 'the sense o a human steer ye couldna read up'.

But it is his grandfather's nieve (fist) that sticks in your mind as you read Mackie's prose — a quarryman's nieve, red-veined and hardened by a lifetime's

A twentieth-century sun-worshipper sits at the feet of a 19th-century duke. This statue of George, 5th and last Duke of Gordon, who raised the Gordon Highlanders, was erected in the Castlegate in 1842— the first granite statue in Scotland. The Circuit judge Lord Cockburn thought it was 'a bad statue, but very ornamental of a street'. It was moved to Golden Square in 1952. Here, in the middle of a crowded parking area, it seems a good deal less ornamental.

work in granite. 'In yon auld man's nieve grippin his luntin bouwl (pipe),' he wrote, 'I sea the biggin o the haill toun. Him and his like for mair nor a hunner year haed quarried the foonds of a city and raised it to the fower airts.' 'My Grandfather's Nieve' is an essay on a way of life chipped out of the granite heart of Rubislaw Quarry. It has gone now, and all that is left is a fenced-in 500ft hole, a tomb in which to bury the past.

There used to be a familiar saying, 'Meet me at the Queen'. The Queen was Queen Victoria and the meeting place was the south-east corner of St Nicholas Street. The first statue of Victoria was erected there in 1866, but was removed to the Town House in 1888. Its successor was erected in 1893, but in 1964 it was moved to Queen's Cross. Now, as the picture shows, her Majesty gazes wistfully up Queen's Road towards Balmoral.

When you think of Aberdeen and its stone, you think of the genius of Simpson and Smith, of Union Street and the granite splendour of the Music Hall. You think of the posh mansion houses of Queen's Road and Rubislaw Den, and the 'twirlie-wirlies' of Marischal College, which was once called both a miracle in granite and a miracle in bad taste. But there is another side to the Granite City. 'Whit did ye bigg, granda?' asked Alastair Mackie. 'The sillert mansions o Rubislaw and Mannofield; the twisted crunny and orra stink o Crooked Lane, the brookit tenements o Black's Buildings, the Denburn, the Gallowgate, East North Street and West North Street...'

It has always seemed to me that Aberdeen is a tenement town. The tenements of today are products of the granite age, although there were tenements of one kind or another long before the first stone was cut at Rubislaw. The original heart of Aberdeen's granite industry was actually at the Loanhead quarry in the Rosemount district, which opened in 1730, a decade before quarrying began at Rubislaw. In 1775, Samuel Johnson visited the city and commented on its 'large and lofty' houses. 'They build almost wholly with the granite used in the new pavement of the streets of London, which is well known not to want hardness, yet they shape it easily,' wrote Johnson. 'It is beautiful and must be very lasting.' Large and lofty they may have been, but Aberdeen tenement blocks never reached the height of those in Glasgow or Edinburgh, where they boasted buildings of seven or more storeys. Parson Gordon's three or four storeys struck the right average.

Tenements ranged up and down the social scale, depending on which part of the city you lived, and even within particular districts there were startling contrasts. I was brought up in a three-storey tenement in Wallfield Place (immortalised in Harry Gordon's 'Wallfield, Nellfield, Manofield and Cattofield...'), and in the social stakes it was probably regarded as a 'better class' of tenement. John Souter, who was senior assistant with Aberdeen District Council's planning department, once told me that there was a great deal of snobbery in tenements, and he was right. He remembered a woman in Willowbank boasting that there were police sergeants and tramway inspectors in her street, which clearly made it a cut above the rest. Wallfield must have been in the same category, for there were at least half a dozen 'bobbies' there, including my father, whose helmet and baton always hung in the lobby to scare off undesirables.

Gaslight guttered on the stairs of the Wallfield tenement, as well as inside the house. The rules were spelled out in framed notices in the ground-floor lobby, so that you knew when it was your turn to polish the communal linoleum, when it was your wash-day, and when you could use the loft. There were no bathrooms, only a zinc bath on a Saturday, and if you didn't want to go downstairs to the toilet in the middle of the night you had a chamber-pot under your bed. A 'chuntie', they called it. Yet there were tenements no great distance away where there were shared sinks on the stairs or a water tap at the back-door. Davie Duncan, who lived in Minister Lane, off Summer Street, recalled in *Tenements and Sentiments* that children from a better type of neighbourhood, who could afford pennies to buy sweeties, were a race apart.

The Shiprow, said John Souter, was said to be the worst tenement area. Disease was rife, particularly consumption, caused by the appalling overcrowding. He had a photograph, taken in 1898, which was an interesting reminder of how some people escaped from this miserable existence in an East End tenement. It showed a smartly-dressed Victorian woman wearing an ostrich feather hat and a dress with leg-of-mutton sleeves, while beside her, standing on a seat, was a small boy with button-up gaiters and a stick in his hand. The boy was John Souter's father; the woman, his grandmother. She was one of thirteen of a family living in a tenement at 81 Wales Street, where they slept six to a bed. The photograph was taken after his grandmother, who

The glitter of granite in the city's west end...an impressive example of the use of granite in a building not far from Rubislaw Quarry. This house at 50 Queen's Road was the home of John Morgan, the builder, who, among other things, was involved in the laying out of Union Terrace Gardens and the building of the Public Library. It replaced Rubislaw House, the house of the Skenes of Rubislaw, which was taken down in 1886. Morgan called it 'the new House of Rubislaw'.

was married and widowed by the age of twenty-four, had moved to King Street.

Most of the Victorian tenements in Aberdeen have been modernised, but some have vanished, among them Alastair Mackie's 'brookit tenements' in Black's Buildings, on the south side of Woolmanhill. These tenements, which rose to four and five storeys, were built between 1798 and 1830 by James Black, a wine merchant, who was nicknamed the Black Prince. The whole block was demolished in 1957. Black's Buildings ended their days as a slum, yet at one time they held a better class of tenant than any other houses in the surrounding streets.

Alastair Mackie was born in Baker Street, but not in a tenement, although he was surrounded by tenements. There was a distillery there in 1760, converted into a brewery six years later. At the opposite side of Rosemount Viaduct from Baker Street a collection of old tenements, their windows boarded up, set out the line of Stevenson Street, which, running parallel to the Viaduct, dropped down below its level and seemed to disappear underground. It was known as the Incurable Brae (a hospital for incurable diseases stood there), and towards the end of the nineteenth century a hotel — the Imperial Hotel — was planned for this tawdry corner of Rosemount.

If things had been different the hotel would have stood on one of Aberdeen's main thoroughfares, for Stevenson Street, which turns into the Upper Denburn at the foot of Jack's Brae, was considered as a possible direct route between the Denburn district and Rosemount. Instead, Rosemount Viaduct was built and Stevenson Street became a forgotten backwater.

Not much thought is given to why Rosemount Viaduct got its name, yet it was a vital piece of the jigsaw that grew into the Aberdeen that we know today. The population of Rosemount expanded rapidly, but the district had no proper access from the centre of the city. The popular way was by Skene Square, which was too indirect, or by the Upper Denburn, Jack's Brae and Short Loanings. The laying out of Esslemont Avenue, where tenements climb up the steep brae to Rosemount Place, provided part of the answer.

The building of a Viaduct over the Denburn Valley was the final solution. The plan, although not as revolutionary as the Union Bridge scheme, was ambitious and costly, with the Viaduct first crossing the Denburn Valley railway to the north end of Union Terrace, then spanning the Upper Denburn by a series of arches to the south end of South Mount Street.

It was the Rosemount Viaduct development in 1883 that opened up the north-west side of the city. It also spawned the tall tenements lining the Viaduct. Rising to five or six storeys, their full height can be seen from the Upper Denburn, where they drop below the level of Rosemount Viaduct. Here, too, are the brick outlines of the stairhead lavatories that were a feature of the old city tenements. The last block of tenements planned before the last war was Rosemount Square, where Cocky Hunter's store once stood. It was completed in 1945–46, and it virtually marked the end of the tenement era.

Glasgow turned one of its old tenements into a museum, Aberdeen thought about it and did nothing. It is a pity, because tenement life in the Granite City will be forgotten in the twenty-first century. Glasgow has its own tenement literature, but not much has been written about Aberdeen's tenements. There will be nothing to show how it was when life was a sink at the window, a bed recess in the corner, and a shared 'lavie' on the landing.

The high granite tenements of Torry, with a horse and cart, a car and a motor bus the only traffic on the steep brae of Victoria Road. Today, it is a busy thoroughfare, running down to Victoria Bridge and Aberdeen. Torry folk have always regarded themselves as a race apart from the 'toonsers' across the water. Picture by courtesy of Aberdeen City Libraries.

The back-green — the 'backie' — was the pivot of life in a tenement. The coal-cellars were there, and sometimes the outside toilets, and it was there that street musicians sang in the hope that some soft-hearted housewife would fling down a penny to them. In the wash-house, its boiler lit at five o'clock in the morning, steaming and bubbling, clothes were heaved out of the tub with a big, heavy stick and a fearsome iron mangle with huge wooden rollers waited in the corner to finish the job. Later, socks and 'semits', 'sarks' and long drawers fluttered from the clothes line like bunting or hung from the long wooden poles sticking out from tenement windows.

There were times when life in a tenement left a lot to be desired, especially when you were hard put to pay the rent, but you always consoled yourself with the thought that things could be worse. Pawky wee Tommy Mitchell, who was Boxmaster to the Bakers' Corporation before he became Lord Provost and *Sir* Thomas Mitchell, obviously thought that tenement-dwellers should look on the bright side. There was a story told about how, as Boxmaster, he went to a tenement in Union Grove to collect the rent and was met by a stream of complaints.

Times were bad, said the housewife, the rent was too high, repairs hadn't been done, and there wasn't any money coming in.

'There!' she said, jabbing her finger at a row of patched and shabby washing on the clothes line outside. 'Look oot there! Look at a' these lang drawers an nae airses!'

Tommy took a look out of the window and said, 'It could have been worse.'

'Fit wye could it hiv been worse?' asked the housewife bitterly.

'Well,' said Tommy philosophically, 'it could hiv been a' airses an' nae lang drawers!'

CHAPTER FOUR
Beleaguered City

The city is closing in on the old St Fittick's churchyard at Nigg, creeping up on it as it stands forlornly on the edge of the vast Balnagask housing estate. The ruined kirk, with its leper's squint and ancient belfry, looks down on the Bay of Nigg. There is a walled graveyard, full of lurching tombstones, and on the gable end of the church, smothered in ivy, a stone has been erected to the memory of Charles Gibbon, Merchant in Aberdeen, who died on 17 of September, 1800. That was the time of the body-snatchers.

On a bleak December night in 1808 the corpse of an old woman called Janet Young was dug from its grave in St Fittick's and carried away. Pieces of coffin lid and tattered strips of linen were left on the ground. There was blood on the earth. In February, 1809, another grave was robbed. The body-snatchers, disturbed in their grisly work, buried the corpse in the sand on the north side of the bay, but a storm raised it and carried it over to the south side, where it was found by relatives. Later, it was discovered that the leader of the body-snatchers was a medical student — 'a forward, impudent, not well behaved young man, a student-in-physic', who later fled the country.

The plundering of graves was not confined to Nigg. The Mither Kirk of St Nicholas, St Machar's Cathedral, the Spital and St Clement's kirkyards were all raided by 'Resurrectionists'. Long before Burke and Hare plied their murderous trade in Edinburgh, Aberdeen led the field in the macabre business of body-snatching. In 1801, Charles Jameson was convicted of stealing the body of James Marr, a miller, from the Spital churchyard. He was bound over in his father's surety of £50. Like the impudent grave-robber of Nigg, he was a medical student, but what was hushed up at the time was the fact that he was also secretary of the Aberdeen Medical Society, which later became the Aberdeen Medico-Chirurgical Society.

The Medical Society was to all intents and purposes a body-snatching organisation. It was set up in 1789 by a group of medical students who were dissatisfied with the teaching of medicine and irked by the lack of proper facilities for the study of anatomy. Ostensibly, its main function was to arrange lectures by the town's doctors and surgeons, but it took on board a more dubious role. When six of its former members met in London in 1794, they sent a message back to their colleagues — 'Bodies are procured in London for dissection almost every day. We leave anyone to form their opinion whether it would not be an easier affair in Aberdeen.'

It was a message that was well heeded. Now, the Society that nurtured the Resurrectionist movement has passed its bicentenary. Those founder members lived in an age when change was sweeping through Europe. In their own eyes they were the pioneers of late eighteenth- and early nineteenth-century medicine, but they sought progress down new and dangerous alleys. Nevertheless, the organisation they formed became a powerful force in the advance of medicine in Aberdeen.

In those restless days two names stood out from the crowd. One was that of James McGrigor, son of an Aberdeen merchant, who was a leading figure in the setting up of the Medical Society. Sir James McGrigor, as he became, was founder of the Army Medical Corps. A tall, red-granite obelisk on the south side of the Duthie Park commemorates his work as a military surgeon. It originally stood in front of Marischal College.

The other name was that of Andrew Moir, a lecturer in anatomy, who often led his students on resurrection raids. He was a well-liked teacher, but he was less popular with the public, who were highly suspicious about what went on in his rooms in Flourmill Brae and in the Guestrow, where he had his home. Their fears were fuelled by the Burke and Hare affair and Moir frequently had stones flung at his doors and windows. The anatomist later moved to larger premises in St Andrew Street, and it was there that the city's great 'Burkin' ' scandal erupted.

Aberdeen, which seems to have been afflicted by various 'pongs' over the years, probably never had one quite as bad as the stench wafting from the anatomical theatre in 1831. It was caused by the careless burial of human remains. About two o'clock on a December afternoon, a group of children playing near the theatre watched with horror as a dog, scraping at the earth behind the building, dragged out mangled pieces of a human body.

When the alarm was raised a crowd gathered and other remains were found. The infuriated mob burst into the theatre and the anatomist and his students were chased from the building. Moir was pursued as far as his own home. He is said to have jumped through a window of his house and escaped through St Nicholas churchyard. Three bodies partly dissected were carried to Drum's Aisle in St Nicholas Church. Meanwhile, the mob ransacked the building and set fire to it.

The outcome was that three men were arrested and charged with setting fire to the anatomical theatre and assaulting Moir and a medical student called James Polson. One of the accused said he had gone to the spot to see if he could find the body of his grandmother, who had been interred a few weeks earlier. Each was jailed for twelve months.

For Moir, however, the matter was far from over. He was to Aberdeen what Burke and Hare's patron, Dr Robert Knox, was to Edinburgh; perhaps even worse in the public's eye, for Knox never went out body-snatching, nor did he

encourage his students to rob graves. Moir, a gentle man, who had once contemplated entering the Church, became an object of contempt. His students were pestered and threatened and visitors to his house were pelted with garbage.

With the passing of the Anatomy Act in 1832 Moir could work in relative peace. He was given a lecturer's position at King's College in 1839 and received an honorary degree of MD in the following year, but he was never able to shrug off a sense of bitterness at his treatment. In 1844 he contracted typhoid fever from a patient and died at the early age of thirty-eight. Whatever the public thought of him, his colleagues in the Aberdeen Medico-Chirurgical Society respected both the man and his work. His funeral started from the society's Medical Hall, the stately building, designed by Archibald Simpson, whose Ionic portico dominates the south end of King Street. Today, the Customs and Excise have taken over the old hall, leaving no trace of what happened behind those impressive granite columns in the days of the Resurrectionists.

He was buried in St Nicholas churchyard — the Town Churchyard — and a large crumbling tombstone marks his last resting place — Andrew Moir, Lecturer on Anatomy, King's College Medical School. There is a touch of irony in the fact that it was in the town kirkyard, fleeing from a howling mob, that he is said to have hidden — under a tombstone.

St Andrew Street, scene of the Burkin' scandal, was originally called Hospital Row because it ran down to the hospital at Woolmanhill. The south block at Woolmanhill was the work of Archibald Simpson, who designed the Medico-Chirurgical Society's headquarters in King Street some twenty years earlier. Woolmanhill is a name that is grafted in the minds of generations of Aberdonians; it means hospital clinics, doctors, out-patients and casualties.

Woolmanhill is not generally spoken of as Aberdeen Royal Infirmary. For many years, and particularly in the post-war period, it was regarded simply as an out-patients' annexe to the Foresterhill complex. Nevertheless, the neo-classical block at Woolmanhill, said to be one of Archibald Simpson's most successful projects, was the *first* Royal Infirmary. Nowadays, it sometimes is still referred to as the old Royal Infirmary.

The decision to build a hospital at Woolmanhill was taken in 1739, although it was 1741 before it was erected. It was demolished and replaced in 1840 by the new south block. The original buildings were erected at a cost of £484

The familiar spire of St Nicholas Church, the Mither Kirk of Aberdeen. The church, divided since the Reformation into two separate places of worship, the East and West Churches, was first mentioned in a papal bull of 1157. The West Church, originally the nave, was rebuilt in the middle of the 18th century by the well-known architect James Gibbs. The long table tombstone in the foreground marks the grave of Andrew Moir, lecturer in anatomy, whose resurrectionist activities raised the wrath of local people. He was chased by a mob and escaped through St Nicholas Churchyard, hiding under a tombstone.

Tombstones cast dark shadows over the grounds of St Fittick's Church at Nigg. The kirkyard at St Fittick's was a target for body-snatchers in the early 19th century. The building in the corner was a Watch-house, where relatives and friends sheltered when standing guard over the graves. Another kind of violence is recalled in a grave-slab telling how a Kincorth man, William Milne, 'fell by the sword of a savage Irishman' during the Covenanting troubles.

(Simpson's new block cost £16,700 and had 230 beds) and the plan was to accommodate twenty people 'sick in body and mind'. Those sick in mind were housed in six gloomy rooms which were described as 'very good Bedlam Cells'. One of the first patients was a young woman who was 'chained and bound' and had 'a strong man set over her'.

The Aberdeen Royal Mental Hospital that we know today grew from 'a Bedlam' — the original asylum at Clerkseat, in the Berryden and Elmhill area. It was opened in 1800 and had twelve cells, each 8ft. by 8ft. 6in. The Cornhill hospital has for long had a reputation for forward thinking in the treatment of mental patients, but it had murky beginnings. Equipment for restraining patients included ankle straps, straitjackets, iron handcuffs, muzzles and a 'hand barrow for moving patients'. There was also a fiendish rotatory chair for quietening them. It was rotated fifty or a hundred times a minute and reversed every six or eight minutes. The usual result was that the patient emptied his bowels and bladder before passing out.

Along the Lang Stracht, only a mile or two from the Royal Mental Hospital and the Royal Infirmary, is Woodend Hospital, which, although complementary to Foresterhill, has always seemed to be set apart from it. It has never quite been able to shake off its origins, for it was originally a boys' reformatory and later a poorhouse. Officially, it was called Oldmill Hospital when it opened in 1907, but it catered mostly for the 'sick poor'. Not so many years before the last war people had a dread of landing up in 'the Poorshoose'. It was taken over by the Town Council and renamed Woodend Hospital in 1927.

By the 1920s, when new ideas on health care were taking root, a project known as the Joint Hospitals Scheme came under discussion. The plan was that a new hospital would be built embracing all aspects of hospital care, plus a medical school. The man behind the Joint Hospital Scheme was Professor Matthew Hay, who was Aberdeen's Medical Officer of Health for thirty-five years and Professor of Forensic Medicine at Aberdeen University. In 1920, Hay put his plan before the Medico-Chirurgical Society and in 1927, an appeal for £400,000 was launched by Lord Provost (later Sir) Andrew Lewis. When it closed, £407,000 had been subscribed.

The site for the new buildings was on the outskirts of the town, near Burnside, where the old Stocket Forest once spread itself across Stocket Hill. Long before his plan had even been considered, Matthew Hay had earmarked the slopes of Foresterhill as the ideal spot for his dream hospital complex. When the go-ahead was given it had already been decided that the buildings would be granite, for the folk of the Granite City had made it clear that that was what they wanted. In September, 1936, the new Aberdeen Royal Infirmary was opened by the Duke of York, accompanied by the Duchess of York, now the Queen Mother.

The 'Sick Kids' beat the adults in the race to Foresterhill. The hospital, opened on Castlehill in 1877, moved to its new site in 1928. Later, the maternity hospital and the medical school followed suit and became the final pieces in Matthew Hay's ambitious jigsaw.

The old Royal Infirmary at Woolmanhill is still in use, but the majority of its departments have moved to Foresterhill. People were going to Woolmanhill to cure themselves of their ills four centuries ago, but there was no hospital then — only a well. Aberdeen has had its share of wells, some offering 'miracle' cures, others simply places where people could quench their thirst. There was the Firhill Well, which people flocked to on Sunday mornings in summer, and the Boathouse Brae Well at Kittybrewster, near the old Canal, and others less well-known like the Gilcomston Brewery Well, the Angel Well, near Hanover Street, and the Thieves' Brig Well in Park Street.

With its four Greek Ionic columns, this building in King Street is reminiscent of the Music Hall. Both were designed by Archibald Simpson, but the building above appeared a few years before Simpson's Assembly Rooms in Union Street. It was built in 1818–20 for the Aberdeen Medico-Chirurgical Society. The society, founded in 1789, wanted it as a meeting place and to house their library, but it was also a centre for less respectable insurrectionist activities. Today, it houses the offices of the Customs and Excise.

Many have disappeared, but the old Spa Well, which once stood in the Four-neukit Garden, near where the west gable of the old Royal Infirmary can now be seen, is still around. It is only a few steps from the Denburn car park. Its chalybeate waters (containing iron) were thought to have curative powers in the sixteenth century, when Dr Gilbert Skene, King James VI's doctor, wrote a pamphlet about the beneficial effects of drinking from the weld. In 1635, when the Aberdeen artist George Jamesone laid out his Four-neukit Garden in the Playfield at Woolmanhill — and gave the city its first public park — he repaired the Spa Well so that it would 'withstand the violence of speattis in tyme cuming'.

A well-known physician, Dr William Barclay, who analysed its waters, was suitably impressed, and wrote a treatise on 'What diseases may be cured by drinking of the Well at Aberdene, and what is the true use thereof'. The tract was reprinted in 1670 and again in 1799, when Dr Barclay took a swipe in verse at people who favoured the waters of the Firhill Well:

> The blessing, Health, whoever truly lacks,
> Will soon perceive the fallacy of Quacks,
> Not but I grant the Firhill Well is rich
> In Sulphur, which may serve to cure the Itch;
> But has it those restoring, bracing powers
> Which Barclay amply proves are found in ours?
> It may, but if it has, they're still to find,
> While Spa's great Cures are known to half mankind.

The well ceased to be a water supply point towards the end of last century, but in 1977 it was re-erected, with its original flanking seats restored, on its present site.

The enterprising Dr Barclay had another sure cure for your ailments — tobacco. There was no nonsense about lung cancer and heart disease from this practitioner. He believed that tobacco got rid of asthma, ulcers, shortness of breath, coughs, ulcers, wounds, migraine, colic, paralysis, epilepsy, apoplexy... even an embarrassing attack of 'dizziness in the head by wind'. 'Yea, almost all diseases,' declared the doctor. He wrote a tract *The Virtues of Tobacco* in which he put forward tobacco as a panacea for all ills. 'It hath certaine mellifluous delicacie which deliteth the senses and spirits of man with a mindful oblivion, insomuch that it maketh and induceth the forgetting of all sorrowes and miseries.'

It would have taken more than tobacco to rid Aberdeen of the sorrows and miseries that afflicted it four or five centuries ago. Leprosy, syphilis, dysentery, smallpox and cholera were among the diseases our forefathers had to contend with. There was a leper house near what is now the east end of Nelson Street. The last case of leprosy seems to have been in 1604, when 'ane puir woman infectit with Leprosie' was put in a hospital 'betwixt the townis'; in other words, between Old and New Aberdeen.

Worst of all the city's 'sorrows and miseries' was the plague or pestilence, which struck at Aberdeen with fearful regularity. The Black Death came in 1350 and in 1401 there was the first recorded outbreak of 'the pest'. There were six outbreaks in the first half of the sixteenth century. The nature of the disease has never been clear, but it is thought that it may have been typhus or paratyphoid. The Council Register described the 1539 outbreak as 'the contagious infecting pest called the boiche', and it has been said that this was the plague. The Botch resulted in an eruptive, discoloured swelling on the skin.

The disease spread like wildfire, largely because of the totally inadequate sanitary arrangements in the town. While little was done about the reeking heaps of filth that piled up in the streets, the City Fathers took other action to

The Spa Well, famed for its 'miracle' waters as far back as the Middle Ages. 'Spa's great cures are known to half mankind,' wrote Dr William Barclay, a well-known physician, early in the 17th century. The well ceased to be used as a water supply point after the 1860s. It was re-erected in its present site near the Denburn Centre in 1977.

halt the plague. Stray dogs were destroyed, swine were no longer allowed to wander about the streets, and beggars were thrown out of town. As fear and panic spread among the population, there were reports of parents abandoning their plague-stricken children, and even of children abandoning their parents. In 1546, a father was branded with a hot iron for concealing his child's sickness, and the bailies warned that future offenders would be hanged.

Hanging was a familiar remedy. During the 1585 outbreak, three gibbets were erected, one at the Market Cross, another at the Bridge of Dee, and the third at the harbour mouth. If an 'infectit person' turned up in the burgh he was liable to be strung up, and if any of the townsfolk gave shelter to someone suffering from the plague, or provided him with meat and drink, the magistrates' instructions were that 'the man be hangit and the woman drownit'.

Despite such stringent precautions, a plague victim slipped through the net in 1647. In April, the magistrates were told that a case of pestilence had been reported at Bervie. Steps were taken to ensure that nobody from that area entered the town, but a short time later it was discovered that two members of a family living at Pitmuckston (near Allenvale Cemetery) had died from the disease. It had been brought in from Brechin. What was even worse was the fact that one of the children had been attending an English school in the burgh.

It was the start of the worst outbreak of plague ever to ravage Aberdeen. Four months later, more than 1700 people were dead, one quarter of the population. The council struggled desperately to contain the epidemic. All dogs and cats were killed, poison was laid for mice and rattons (rats), and hawkers of clothes were forbidden to carry on their business. The better class of citizen had to stay in his house until it was 'clengit' — disinfected. Council meetings were cancelled, and when members reassembled for urgent business they met at Woolmanhill, which was then outside the burgh boundary. Later, an election was held even farther afield at the Crofts of Gilcomston.

People infected with the disease, or likely to have caught it, were isolated from the community and sent off to encampments at the Links and Gallowhill, where wooden huts were built to accommodate them. They were known as the Lodges. In effect, they were death camps, for the majority of patients who went there died. They were burned or buried in pits and trenches near the huts. The largest of the mass graves was east of York Street. Some of the graves of Lodges' victims were found late last century when a sewer was laid through the Links.

Military guards were on duty to keep victims in and visitors out. The Treasury and Guildry Accounts of the period show that one of the highest payments was £820 11s 0d — 'To Captain John Duff and the military for guards'. Apart from money for food, the highest item of expense was £1086 10s 0d — 'To James Graham, cleanger, for his services and attendance on the people'. Cleangers or clengers were disinfecters, and their task was to disinfect both places and people. The accounts also showed the entry — 'To expence of a double tree for a gibbet, and for erecting it — £2 15s 0d'. It was a grim reminder that if they tried to escape one form of death another awaited them at the entrance to the Lodges. They were executed on the spot.

The 1647 epidemic was said to be the last outbreak of plague in Aberdeen, and there were certainly no more epidemics of such proportions. But three centuries later history repeated itself. In May, 1964, the city reeled under a typhoid fever outbreak which almost brought it to a halt. There were 500 cases of typhoid and only one person died, an elderly woman whose death was not directly attributable to the disease. It was a minor epidemic compared to the great plagues of the past, yet news of the outbreak spread abroad and for a time made people shun the Granite City.

A building known to generations of Aberdonians simply as 'Woolmanhill'. The Old Infirmary was designed by Archibald Simpson between 1832 and 1839 and was regarded as one of his most successful architectural projects. The hospital at Woolmanhill included buildings to the north, but these have now been emptied by a general move to Foresterhill. The south block the Old Infirmary — is still in use.

There were some peculiar parallels with the past. The victims were sent off to the Links, just as they were 300 years earlier, but this time the 'Lodges' were the wards of the City (Fever) Hospital. Not only that, the hospital actually stood on the site at the Links where Lodges were built during the plague epidemic of 1647. The Broad Hill area was known then as the Cunningar Hills (the word means a rabbit warren) and the hospital was often called by that name.

It was known as Cunningarhill hospital when it was built in 1877, following a bill giving local authorities certain powers to deal with infectious diseases. When Professor Matthew Hay, the city's Medical Officer of Health, took it over it was a seedy and unpopular place, but he renovated and extended it and raised its reputation to the high level that it still holds today. It was to be tested, and not found wanting, when in 1964 a 7lb. tin of bad corned beef put Aberdeen on the map as the Typhoid City.

A picture that told the world that Aberdeen, the Beleaguered City, was back in business again.
It got the unwelcome title when an outbreak of typhoid in May, 1964, filled the wards at the
City Hospital, brought business to a halt, and virtually wiped out the holiday trade. Nobody
wanted to come to Aberdeen. When the city was given the all-clear a month later, the Queen,
who was on the Royal yacht Britannia in the Moray Firth, paid an unexpected visit to
Aberdeen to put her Royal stamp on the city's return to normality. Our picture shows her
talking to one of the nurses who helped to fight the outbreak. Picture by courtesy of Aberdeen
Journals.

The man at the centre of this modern 'plague' was a balding, pipe-smoking
Medical Officer of Health called Dr Ian A.G. MacQueen. Unlike most council
officials, he was always happy to talk to the Press. With an epidemic on his
hands, he wanted to get his message over to the public. He had a turn of phrase
that delighted news-hungry reporters — and he grabbed the headlines. After
one of his Press conferences, Aberdonians picked up their newspapers to see

splashed across the front page the words BELEAGUERED CITY. It was a headline that appeared in newspapers all over the world.

Dr MacQueen may have overstated the case, and he came in for criticism because of it, but in a sense Aberdeen *was* a beleaguered city. Cinemas, dance halls and bingo halls had to put up their shutters. Schools were closed and there was even talk of closing the city's pubs, but Dr MacQueen said he didn't want to turn Aberdeen into a monastery. Business slumped and hotels were inundated with calls from people cancelling their holiday bookings. Aberdonians had to cancel their own holidays; fearful landladies in the south made it clear they didn't want visitors from Typhoid City.

Not surprisingly, some newspapers went over the top. One paper described Aberdeen as a City of Fear, and a Spanish publication reported that the city's dead were being gathered in the streets and thrown into the sea. It was said that Aberdeen was the place where no one was allowed to enter or leave — shades of 1647!

The myth of the mean Aberdonian came alive on the back of the epidemic. An Aberdeen mother wrote to the *Evening Express* complaining that her schoolgirl daughter had used a toilet at the Beach and, after washing her hands, had dried them with her own paper towel. She was then charged threepence for the use of the basin. 'In Aberdeen,' commented the aggrieved mother, 'the motto seems to be, "If you want hygiene, 3d extra".' The hygiene-conscious council quickly put a halt to this sort of thing. Parsimonious Aberdonians found that they didn't even have to spend a penny — they could use public loos free of charge.

The first suspects were admitted to the City Hospital on 20 May and a team of experts — doctors, bacteriologists, health visitors, meat inspectors, sanitary department inspectors and a host of others — went into action to trace the source of the outbreak. They came up with the answer in three days — the outbreak came from infected corned beef in a big Aberdeen store.

A month later the city was given the all-clear. On 20 June the first typhoid victim was released from hospital. She was Evelyn 'Bobby' Gauld, a librarian, who had been admitted to Tor-na-Dee Hospital when the City Hospital became jammed with typhoid cases. When she left Tor-na-Dee the staff gave her a sash with the inscription, 'Typhoid Queen, 1964'.

The real Queen, who was on the Royal yacht *Britannia* in the Moray Firth, paid an unexpected visit to Aberdeen on 28 June, putting her Royal stamp on the city's return to normality. Fifty thousand people turned out to greet her. After that, shops became busy again, tomatoes and lettuce came off the banned list, hotels reported that holidays were being re-booked, and tearooms and restaurants began to do brisk business. But it was a long time before corned beef came back on the menu in the Granite City.

The Botch, the Plague, the idea of converting a coal cellar into cells for

A helicopter drops down on to a landing pad in the grounds of Aberdeen Royal Infirmary at Foresterhill. This has become a common sight in the years of the oil boom. Many of the patients in the 'choppers' are sick and injured workers from the oil rigs. During the Piper Alpha disaster, a helicopter shuttle service ran through the night carrying victims from the rig to the hospital.

mental patients...these things seem to belong to a nightmarish past that we can scarcely imagine. Now there are kidney machines, body scanners, heart transplants, and aids and techniques that a century ago would have been regarded as something out of the fevered mind of a 'Bedlamite'. The helicopter pad at Foresterhill is regarded with scarcely more interest than the bus stop over the infirmary wall, yet during the Piper Alpha disaster the 'choppers' came drumming out of the darkness all night with victims from the stricken oil rig. Perhaps we take progress with too much equanimity.

The coming of the new Millennium brought a rash of speculation about the future of the Health Service. For the past decade, Grampian Health Board have been planning for the new century. In 1927, Professor Matthew Hay's imaginative Joint Hospital Scheme was launched with an appeal for £400,000. In 1989. it was reckoned that the money required for a plan to take the hospital service into the twenty-first century would be £14 million.

Developments at the start of 1998 suggested that the figure would go well beyond that. It was announced that there would be a mayor £22 million redevelopment of health facilities on the Foresterhill site. A new children's hospital would be built by the year 2003 and there would be a new out-patient department and day-case surgery unit.

But the major signpost to the future lay up on the Foresterhill skyline. There, early in 1998, the building housing the new Institute of Medical Sciences was nearing completion. It was the final moves in what Professor Graeme R.D. Catto, Dean of the Medical School, galled an 'exciting initiative'. The plan was to move more than 180 researchers into the Institute, followed by senior research students. The first suite of laboratories would be occupied by research teams interested in aspects of molecular biology, then clinical scientists involved in such things as auto-immune disorders, genetics and oncology, and finally neuroscientists with interests in molecular pharmacology.

Medicine had come a long way since Dr Richard Barclay had proclaimed that 'drinking of the Well at Aberdene' would cure most disseases — and that 'Spa's great Cures are known to half mankind'.

CHAPTER FIVE
Whalers and Clippers

Ｉn the long-forgotten days when whalers pummelled their way through the icy wastes of the Arctic to bring their cargoes of blubber and whalebone back to Aberdeen, they came home to a familiar huddle of cottages at Waterside of Fittie, where huge arches made from whalebone jaws rose above the bleach greens. The jawbones, relics of earlier trips to Greenland and the Davis Straits, were used as gateposts. They were 25ft. long, big enough to take a waggonload of hay. The whalers came up the Raick to Pocra jetty, passing the thick rubble walls of the old Blockhouse, which had been turned into a boiling-house for the production of whale oil.

From the shore, the folk of Fittie could hear the chant of a sea shanty as the ships were hauled up the entrance channel:

> We'll go in to Jean Mackenzie's,
> And buy a pint o' gin,
> And drink it on the jetty,
> When the *Jane* comes in.

The Jane was a 278-ton whale ship built in 1797. In 1810, returning from Greenland, she sailed into Aberdeen with one of the biggest cargoes ever landed at the port — seventeen whales, which produced more than 200 tons of oil. Customs documents of the time mention the arrival of the *Jane* with '383 casks and parcel in bulk', and the *Aberdeen Journal* reported that the vessel's voyage had been so successful that the skipper, Captain Jamson, 'gave one fish and one half to another ship he met with'. The *Jane* arrived home to a triumphant welcome. In the years that followed, her epic voyage was remembered in the shanty sung on whaleships returning from the Arctic.

Those were the years of Aberdeen's *first* oil boom. Oil was as important then as it is now, but in a different way. Whale oil was essential to the economy, for it was used in street lamps, in soap-making, for dressing wool and vegetable fibres, in currying leather and as an industrial lubricant. In 1830 an advertisement appeared in the *Journal* asking for 'Six tons, old weight, of best boiled whale oil for the public lamps of this city'. Wax candles lit the homes of the wealthy, but for those less well-off there was a single tallow candle containing oil from whale blubber, with a rush or cotton wick.

Whalebone, too, was a valuable ancillary product, used by milliners and

The days of the whalers are recalled in this picture of a whalebone arch at the entrance to a bleach green at Waterside of Fittie. It was taken by George Washington Wilson in 1859. Waterside of Fittie was the home of the shipbuilder Alexander Hall. His cottage and yard stood on land which is now part of York Street. Picture by courtesy of Aberdeen City Libraries.

dressmakers — whalebone corsets helped the ladies to keep their hour-glass figures. So, in the second half of the eighteenth century, Aberdeen entered a period of oil prosperity that gave a financial boost to the city's economy and yielded rich dividends to businessmen perceptive enough to jump on the bandwagon. No one could have guessed that history was to repeat itself on a grander scale two hundred years later.

Then, as now, the hunt for oil brought risks as well as rewards. There was the risk of returning to port 'clean', with nothing to show for hazardous months in Arctic waters. The *Bon-Accord,* under the command of John Parker, Aberdeen's top whaling skipper, regularly chalked up huge catches (Parker twice set the city's record of 260 tons of whale oil landed from a single trip), yet in 1836 not a single whale was spotted. The crew even had to borrow oil from another ship to give them light at night until they returned home.

There was also the risk of being stricken by scurvy, starvation and frostbite, or of being trapped and crushed in the ice. Two Aberdeen whalers, the *Middleton* and the *Dee*, with a hundred men and boys on board, were among six vessels frozen in during the winter of 1837. The *Middleton* was crushed and wrecked. The men were taken on board another vessel, but out of a crew of fifty, only twenty survivors got back to Aberdeen. When the *Dee* was released, the captain was dead and her first officer insane. One man held up the bones

The *Cairngorm*, the *Chrysolite*, the *Jerusalem*, the *Phoenician*…they were names that shone like beacons in the golden age of the clipper ships. The greatest of them all was the *Thermopylae*, of 947 tons, which could do the voyage to Melbourne in sixty days, and to Foochow in ninety. Her greatest day's run, an all-time record for sailing ships, was 380 miles. The *Thermopylae* which once brought a signal from a rival captain, 'You are the finest model of a ship I ever saw', is seen above in Sydney harbour. Picture by courtesy of Aberdeen Art Gallery and Museums.

of his toe for inspection. They had been frozen off during the winter and he carried them around in his vest pocket.

Yet there were plenty of volunteers to man the whalers, not least among them youngsters of fourteen to eighteen years of age in search of adventure. In December, 1783, a notice in the *Aberdeen Journal* read: 'Wanted. For a ship to sail from Aberdeen next season, several stout lads as apprentices in the Greenland trade, who have been accustomed to the oar and if they have served at sea, the better.'

The first whale fishing by Aberdeen vessels began in 1752, but it was only moderately successful, and in 1783 the Aberdeen Whaling Company was formed. It had two whalers, the *Hercules* and the *Latona*, and in 1802–3 they were joined by the *Jane* and the *Neptune*. From about 1806, the catches became bigger — in 1807 there were thirteen fish, 'a bumper ship', from the *Neptune* and eighteen fish, 'a full ship', from the *Latona*. In 1810, the year of the *Jane's* big success, the price of oil per ton was £38, and the four ships brought in some 600 tons of oil, adding up to £22,000. Running expenses were below

The days of the tall-masted sailing ships are vividly captured in this picture looking across the Upper Dock at Aberdeen Harbour in the 1870s. In the background is the Upper Quayside, now South Market Street, with its warehouse and slate yards. The sailing ships were a common sight at the head of the Upper Dock. Typical of the smaller sailing ship in use before the age of steel was the wooden three-masted barque City of Aberdeen on the right of the photograph. Its owner was James Tulloch, jun., a well-known Aberdeen merchant and town councillor. Picture by courtesy of Aberdeen City Libraries.

£3,000, leaving a clear profit from the oil alone of £10,000 among the four ships. From 1812 to 1815 three new companies were formed and twelve ships were added to the fleet, bringing the total to sixteen.

But there were losses. In January, 1813, the *Aberdeen Journal* reported that fourteen whalers would sail that year to the Davis Straits and Greenland — 'as fine ships as ever put to sea', it declared proudly. In April, four of them — the *Hercules, Latona, Middleton* and *Oscar* — were riding at anchor in Aberdeen Bay before setting sail for the fishing grounds when a violent storm blew up. The *Oscar*, which was on its second voyage, was driven ashore at Greyhope Bay, just north of Girdle Ness, and completely wrecked. The first mate and a young seaman from Shields were the only survivors of a crew of forty-four. In the same year, the *Latona* was struck by a shoal of ice in the Davis Straits and went down in fifteen minutes.

It was the days of the Zulus and the Fifies, their sails casting crisp patterns against the northern sky. Poets and painters were fascinated by them. The picture above gives meaning to Christopher Rush's lines about 'the dark fins of Fifies' cutting the sky. The Fifies were herring fishing boats first used on the Fife coast, while Zulus, which operated in the Moray Firth about 1880 to 1905, were named after the Zulu War. The red sails of the herring boats are seen vividly in The Herring fleet leaving the Dee a painting by David Farquharson in Aberdeen Art Gallery. Picture by courtesy of Aberdeen City Libraries.

The whalers ranged far into the dangerous Arctic waters. The Greenland waters had been overfished and more and more vessels were heading for the Straits. The year 1825 saw the loss of the *Don,* and in 1829 the Jane, whose whaling feats were still being toasted in Jean Mackenzie's parlour, also went down. Four other Aberdeen vessels were lost in 1830, a disastrous year in which nineteen of the ninety-one British ships at the Davis Straits were lost in the ice and twenty-one returned 'clean' without fish. The great days of whale fishing from Aberdeen were over. The industry went into decline and there were no whaling vessels in the port after 1858. The coming of gas was the final death blow.

Now they were toasting memories, not triumphs, lifting their jugs of grog to an era in which Aberdeen had been Scotland's premier whaling port. Grog

The herring gutters…the girls behind the great herring boom of the 1880s. With more than 450 boats using Aberdeen as their port during the height of the season (from June till the end of September), the gutters were constantly on call. They often worked through the night to gut and pack catches for export to the Baltic. Our picture shows a yard at Point Law in 1883. The large herring farlins (boxes) were often on the open quay and many of the girls, working In cold, salty water, had hacks on their hands that remained open sores until the end of the season. Picture by courtesy of Aberdeen City Libraries.

was a potent combination of Jamaica rum and water — two parts rum, one part water. Captain Lewis Middleton, who sailed with Captain John Parker in the 1830s, told in his *Whaling Recollections* how grog was 'served out as regularly as necessary food'. Drunkenness was rife.

Before they sailed from Aberdeen, the whalers often had to lie out in the Bay while saloons on shore were searched for drunken crew members, who were brought alongside in boats and 'hoisted on deck like so many bales of goods'. Drunkenness brought accidents, and sometimes, tragedy. In 1836, a drunken crew member fell from the main top gallant yard into the sea. 'We jerked him up,' recalled Captain Middleton, 'but he was so badly hurt that he died within a week.'

The loss of the *Oscar* was regarded as an Act of God — one local bard wrote about the raging sea as 'the messenger of God, charged with His dread decree' — but there was a simpler explanation — too much grog. 'The *Oscar* sailed on the first of April,' wrote Captain Middleton, 'and while waiting in the Bay for

The old and the new — sail and steam. This picture of sailing ships and steam vessels in the Albert Basin was taken in 1890. The herring fishing was dominated by sailing vessels in the 1880s and 1890s. The herring drifters in the foreground were in some cases over 60ft in length, with a mast length to equal that. They carried a crew of six or seven. Picture by courtesy of Aberdeen City Libraries.

the Captain, who was detained on Custom House business, an easterly gale came in from seaward. The crew being drunk were unable to handle the ship. She was driven ashore on the Girdleness, became a total wreck, and only the First Mate and one boy were saved.'

The *Eclipse* and the *Hope*, launched at Hall's shipyard in 1866–67 and 1873, were Aberdeen's last Arctic whalers. The *Eclipse* was commanded by Captain David Gray, who came from a famous Peterhead whaling family. She had a chequered career after being sold in 1892. For a time she was with the Russian Imperial Navy, and after the First World War went back to the Arctic as a supply ship. She sank in 1927, was raised in 1929, and became the *Lomonosov*. The old veteran finally met her end in Archangel in 1941, when she was destroyed by a German bomb during an air raid.

The whalers sailed from Pocra Jetty, but laid up for the winter at Poynernook, near what is now the railway station. If there had been good fishing, Pocra suffered from what one writer called 'a pretty strong perfume' from the boilyard. Aberdeen has been plagued by various 'pongs' over the years, but there has been nothing to equal the smell from the Pocra boiling house. As far back as 1784, a letter in the *Aberdeen Journal* complained about the 'intolerable stench' end its effect on the health of the citizens.

There is still a link with the days of whaling — and the 'pong' — in a granite tablet which sits awkwardly on the pavement at Pocra Quay. This is where the old Blockhouse once stood. As the inscription indicates, it was built in 1532, but in 1477 a fort occupied the site. The Blockhouse has served as a place of execution, a watch-tower, a gunpowder store, the Torry ferryman's home — and a boiling-house for whale oil.

The name Pocra is said to be a corruption of 'Pow Creek'. The Powcreek Burn rose in a small spring in West North Street and the old estuary of the burn was the boat harbour of the town until 1658, when it was filled up. The fisher folk of Futtie called it Pockraw, which is said to mean 'the fisher's haven'. That, at anyrate, was what it was for centuries. Old Pocra Quay was built in 1826, but there was a pier there as long ago as 1756. It was from Pocra Quay that fisher wives, bending under loads that took two men to lift on to their backs, carried their fish to the Fish Market. At the turn of the century, a wharf was built at Pocra Jetty for the importation of store cattle from Canada. Now, another century on, oil is back on Pocra. Huge oil supply vessels nudge each other on New Pocra Quay, opposite the Blockhouse stone where the 'perfume' of blubber and whale-oil once filled the air. Silos holding mud and cement for the offshore industry line the quay.

Oil dominates the harbour scene. The old familiar pattern of trawler masts has given way to a jigsaw of cranes and silos. Oil storage tanks stick their brightly-painted thumbs up in the air. Ungainly drillships with derricks and helicopter pads jostle for space with flat-sterned support vessels whose top-heavy appearance makes you wonder about the designer's sense of balance. Aberdeen's seafaring tradition has been turned on its head by the hunt for oil, not least in the physical changes that have taken place in the harbour since the first seismic survey vessels nosed their way into port in the early 1960s.

The Victoria and Upper Docks, originally designed for sailing ships, were reconstructed at a cost of one and a quarter million pounds. New warehouses and office blocks opened up and oil supply bases mushroomed on both sides of the River Dee. Across the water, Old Torry was virtually wiped out by development. The bases were built, initially by the John Wood Group and Seaforth Maritime, to provide specialist facilities for the oil industry, but some were for the exclusive use of individual companies. The port's ninth oil base, formerly the old Herring Market, was opened in 1984. Pocra Quay boasts two oil bases: the reconstructed Harbour Board base opened in 1983 and the private base of Amoco (UK) Exploration Company.

I stood on Pocra Quay and watched the oil boats moving up the navigation

Isie Gaie, one of the fishwives who sold their wares at the Green, wraps up a good 'fry' for a customer. Her box and baskets are laid out near what was originally the rear entrance to Boots, which is now in the St Nicholas Centre. The fisher folk's stances were at the railway end of the Green, away from the crush of farmers around the Mannie o' the Well.

channel — the Raick, they call it. The name means the straight place or fair way. A bulky oil vessel lumbered past, heading for the North Sea oil fields. So many other boats had pushed up this choppy waterway over the years...the drifters, the trawlers, the 'coalie' boats carrying fuel to Aberdeen, the coasters, the fussy little pilot boats and the sma' line fishers, the North boats on their way to Orkney and Shetland, and the London boats, carrying passengers and cargo to the metropolis.

The *Victoria and Albert,* a wooden paddle steamer, clattered into port in 1848 with Queen Victoria and the Prince Consort on board, setting the pattern for more than a century of Royal visits. The first steamship built in Aberdeen, the *Queen of Scotland,* sailed majestically up the channel in 1827 while the band of the Aberdeenshire Militia played 'beautiful airs' to the watching crowd. The

Aberdeen Fish Market in the days of steam trawlers. The Fish Market has always been as much an attraction for visitors as the city's golden sands. In this picture, beyond the rows of fish boxes, the trawlers lie, as H. V. Morton put it, 'as thick as motor-cars at the Derby'. Now the great days are gone and huge oil vessels dominate the harbour scene. Picture by courtesy of Aberdeen City Libraries.

stately clippers came this way, and the tall-masted whalers, following the 'straight place' to the frozen Davis Straits. It must have been an unforgettable sight, for the whale ships usually left on the same day, as many as eight or ten of them. Huge crowds turned up to see *them* off. Captain Lewis Middleton said that a stranger would have thought it was a public holiday. Watching the oil ship go past, I remembered that the day was Friday. No whaler would have sailed on that day a century ago. Never on a Friday. It was unlucky.

It needed more than luck to keep alive the shipbuilding yards of Hall Russell and Co., which lay beyond the Amoco base on Pocra Quay. Faced by a dearth of orders, they struggled to continue a tradition that stretched back to the time when the town council leased four stretches of harbourside at Fittie as space for shipbuilding, and even before that, for there was a shipyard there in 1753. More than two centuries later, Hall Russell's was the sole survivor of an era that made Aberdeen famous in the world of shipbuilding — the last name in a long line of great shipbuilders and great ships. Now it has gone.

The year 1839 was a significant one, for it marked the building of the first Aberdeen clipper, a small, streamlined schooner called the *Scottish Maid*. It was the first of many. The *Scottish Maid* symbolised the leap from old sailing coasters known as 'coffin' ships to wooden clipper ships whose reputation spread across the world as fast as the ships themselves. Among the Aberdeen clippers were legendary names like the *Stornoway,* the *Chrysolite* and the *Cairngorm,* built by Alexander Hall and Company to challenge America in the battle for the China tea trade; and the sturdy *Duthie* ships — *Anne, William, John* and *Alexander* — named after members of the family who built them.

There is a Duthie Room in the Aberdeen Maritime Museum. William Duthie, the founder, ran the first mercantile service between London and Australia and was the first owner to send ships to South America for guano. The Duthie ships may not have received the kind of recognition given to some of the better-known clippers, but they held their own; the *Ann Duthie,* for instance, is said to have twice beaten the famous *Cutty Sark*. The last ship to fly the Duthie flag was the iron four-masted clipper *Port Jackson,* which was built by Alexander Hall.

It was an exciting, romantic period in shipping history and in the forefront was a firm, Walter Hood and Company, whose clippers had names to match the magic of the time…the *Maid of Judah,* the *Ethiopian,* the *Phoenician,* and a clipper ship with a handsome figurehead of Leonidas, the heroic King of Sparta, who was killed in 480BC. It carried the name of the battle in which he died — *Thermopylae.*

Plucking their names from Greek mythology — *Pericles,* for instance after the Athenian statesman responsible for the construction of the Parthenon, and *Salamis,* scene of a naval battle in which the Greeks defeated the Persians — the builders created an aura of greatness around a race of clipper giants that in time were to create their own mythology. The laurel went to the *Thermopylae,* the fastest sailing ship in the world. Her hull was painted sea green, with white lower masts, bowsprits and yardarms, and, like an imperious lady putting a final touch to her make-up, she flaunted gold stripe and gold scroll work.

The *Thermopylae* was built by Hood and Company for Thomson's Aberdeen White Star Line. George Thomson, who was the principal partner in Hood's, was Lord Provost of the city for three years and welcomed Queen Victoria when she disembarked at Aberdeen in 1848 on her way to Balmoral. The *Thermopylae* set off from the Thames on her maiden voyage to Melbourne in November, 1868, and broke the record with a 60-day run from berth to berth. When she arrived at Melbourne she was described as 'the new marvel'.

It was said that she rode out the worst sea like a duck and that when she was going along at 7 knots an hour a man could walk round the decks with a lighted candle. On one occasion, when HMS *Charybdis* attempted to outrun her after leaving Melbourne, she drew away from the warship without any difficulty. 'Goodbye,' signalled the *Charybdis* captain. 'You are too much for us. You are the finest model of a ship I ever saw. It does my heart good to look at you.'

Her fiercest rival was the Clyde-built *Cutty Sark,* and the famous race

A trawler pushes its way up the navigation channel, past the Round House, on its way to the fishing grounds. There wasn't much comfort in these old vessels. When the writer H.V. Morton went to sea on an Aberdeen trawler he said that the sight inside the cabin was 'a sight to make a woman faint'. It was 'just a retreat from wind and rain and sea which men, inured to a harsh life, had carved out for themselves in the bowels of a ship otherwise occupied with 'gear'.' Picture by courtesy of Aberdeen City Libraries.

between the two clippers took place when they were in the China tea trade. They set off for home on the same tide, but during the voyage the *Cutty Sark's* rudder was carried away. The ship's carpenter fitted a temporary rudder, but the delay was too much — the *Thermopylae* arrived home a week ahead of her rival. The last of the great tea clipper races took place in 1870 from Foochow to London, but neither the *Thermopylae* (106 days) nor the *Cutty Sark (110 days)* was able to keep pace with the *Lahloo,* which did it in 97 days.

Still, to the men who built her the *Thermopylae* would always be Cock o' the North. When she arrived at Foochow on her maiden voyage after setting up two records she carried a gilded cock of victory at her masthead. During the night the cock was stolen by a sailor from another clipper, said to be the *Taeping,* another of her bitter rivals. It was never recovered, but it was soon replaced by another golden cock, which stayed there until the end of her life.

The *Thermopylae* flew George Thomson's White Star flag until 1890, when she was sold to a Canadian firm to be used in the rice trade between Burma and Vancouver. Later, the Portuguese Navy bought her as a training ship and renamed her the *Pedro Nunes*. She ended her days as a coaling hulk and in 1907 was hauled out to sea and sunk with full naval honours. It was presumably a final salute to her great days as a clipper, and it would be nice to think that she went to her watery grave with the golden Cock o' the North still glittering on her masthead.

The last clipper to leave the slipway in Aberdeen was the *Caliph*, launched in 1869. By that time the Aberdeen yards were looking ahead to the building of steam trawlers and drifters. The last Aberdeen sailing ship still *afloat is* the *Elissa,* which, while lying as a broken hulk in Piraeus in Greece, was bought by the Galveston Historical Foundation in Texas and towed across the Atlantic. She was rebuilt and re-dedicated in July, 1982. In 1984 a number of old plans of Aberdeen Harbour, along with original drawings, were handed over to the Foundation by John R. Turner, then general manager of Aberdeen Harbour Board.

The *Elissa* was preserved as 'a lasting tribute to the great shipbuilders of Aberdeen'. It seems odd that such a tribute should have been paid on the other side of the Atlantic by the nation that competed against us in the clipper trade. The only thing that Aberdeen can offer is a model of the *Thermopylae* in the Maritime Museum. The museum has been extended by linking Provost Ross's house with the former Trinity Congregational Church.

The name of the *Thermopylae* has lingered on down the years, but not many people remember the *Toiler*. She wasn't much of a boat, just an old wooden, clinker-built paddle tug, almost ready for the scrapheap, yet she sailed into history as the city's first steam trawler. There has never been a more unlikely scenario for the founding of a great industry. The *Toiler*, a converted tug, was bought by a group of Aberdeen businessmen in 1882. In March of that year, on her first trawling trip, she returned to port with three boxes of haddocks, which were sold for £1 17s.

It was a modest start, but the *Toiler* soon showed that trawling meant rich dividends for the owners. For the old tug herself, there was only an ignominious end. She began to leak, her boiler steamed and her engine groaned, and three years after her conversion she was sold for £700. Not long after that her discharge pipe burst and she gurgled to her doom in the waters of the Moray Firth. Ely an odd coincidence, the *Toiler's* oak trawl beam was later fished up by her successor, the *North Star*. It was taken to port and erected at the home of one of her owners, William Pyper, who was regarded as the father of Aberdeen's trawling industry.

Not so long ago people were talking about Aberdeen's long-distance trawl skippers having money in the bank and luxury houses in the city's West End. It wasn't all that different in those early pioneering days. There are accounts of how trawlermen were clearly distinguishable from the old line fishermen at the fish market. The trawlerman wore a bowler hat, jauntily perched on his

The landing of Queen Victoria at Aberdeen on September 8, 1848. The picture shows the Queen and Prince Albert, with three of their children, beneath the massive 'welcome' arch at Aberdeen Harbour. The Royal yacht, Victoria and Albert, sailed in hours ahead of schedule, but the Queen assured Provost George Thomson that the Royal party would disembark at the pre-arranged time. Picture by courtesy of Aberdeen City Libraries.

head, and the heels of his boots were higher than the footwear of ordinary mortals. He liked a good cigar and he usually sported a heavy ring on his finger. There was another outward sign of his wealth. 'There are few misogynists in this walk of life,' said one report, 'and the inamorata of the trawlerman presents a brave show in her sealskins and her gaudily coloured hat.'

At one time, the fish market stood at the foot of the Shiprow, near the Pottie, a deep pool where criminals were drowned. During the herring boom years between 1875 and 1896, hundreds of sailing drifters landed their fish at Point Law, and when trawling displaced herring fishing the first catches were landed at a small wooden jetty at Point Law. In 1889, a new fish market was opened at Commercial Quay, later extended along Albert Quay.

Torry fishermen wanted the market on the south side of the Dee, and in the end the matter had to be settled by a referendum. This community has always had an independent spirit, and still has today, never quite accepting its absorption by the town across the water. To it came the small-line fishers from the coastal villages near Aberdeen, followed at the end of last century by migrants seeking employment in the trawling industry. When Aul' Torry was cleared to make way for oil installations, much of its character was swept away with it. As the Torry poet, Joyce Everill, wrote:

> Nae mair the Torry I kent there,
> Jist ghosts that haunt my mind.

A colourful chapter in the story of Aberdeen's fishing industry was written in the last decade of the nineteenth century. Old pictures show Point Law bustling with life — almost 5000 men and women came to stay in Aberdeen in 1889 to catch and process 92,000 crans of herring — and a painting, *Herring Fleet Leaving the Dee,* by David Farquharson, vividly recaptures the heady atmosphere of that period. It shows the herring drifters pulling away from Point Law, with the wind in their sails. Tall-masted ships lie in Victoria Docks — the last of the clipper ships? — and in the distance are the misty spires of the city and a brooding Aberdeen sky. The picture was painted in 1888 — ten years after that the day of the drifter was over.

The same cycle awaited the trawler. The decline of the trawler fleet was aggravated in the 1970s by National Dock Labour Board restrictions, which meant that the port lost out to other non-scheme ports, although it remained a major centre for processing and marketing. The majority of the inshore fleet boycotted Aberdeen and moved to Peterhead, which since then has enjoyed a remarkable boom. By 1980 the tonnage of fish landed at Aberdeen was the lowest since 1898.

The whalers and the clippers belong to history, but the old trawlers still touch nostalgic chords in the minds of Aberdonians brought up between the wars. Trawling may not have been as tough as whaling, but it was tough enough. 'If you can stick a trawler you can stick anything,' one skipper told the writer H.V. Morton, when he asked to go to sea with him. That was back in 1933, when there were 3000 fishermen on 300 trawlers in Aberdeen. Morton's first impression of a trawler's cabin was overpowering. 'It smelt of men, fish, tobacco, acetylene and Scotch broth,' he said.

There were ten men in the crew. The ordinary members received 9s 6d a day, but there were bonuses of 5s, 7s 6d, and 10s if the catches averaged £30, £40 or £50 a day. Morton drew a chillingly vivid picture of his trip on the trawler. He began by hating her. 'I called her a floating slum. I thought of her as a compromise on a large scale between a clog and a coal bucket. The absence of lavatories and the habit of washing hands in a bucket of water brown with blood and sea slime (and the knowledge that this "fresh" water was filtered and used again and again) revolted me.'

When he left the trawler he was sorry to leave both the boat and its crew.

The compliment he paid Aberdeen's fishermen is still as valid today as it was half a century ago. 'I shall never pass a fish shop again without remembering them and their companions in the little ships that sweep the North Sea day and night,' he wrote. 'For they are as uncomplicated as we in the cities are complicated. They are, in a true sense of the word, sea men.'

Leaping from the Thirties to the Nineties, it is difficult to forecast what will happen in the century ahead. The Harbour Board pinned its hopes for the future on seine-netters and small inshore trawlers. The reconstruction of Commercial Quay West and the fish market was a considerable act of faith. The Queen officially opened the new fish market in August, 1982 — exactly 100 years after a group of far-sighted businessmen had bought the creaking old *Toiler* to make the first experiments in trawling.

CHAPTER SIX
Blyth and Blissful

Aberdeen once boasted its own opera house — Her Majesty's Opera House in Guild Street. It became better known to generations of Aberdonians as the Tivoli, home of a long line of Scots comics, but today its auditorium rings to the cry of 'House!' In the space of little more than a century it has slipped from culture to comedy and, clickety-click, into the role of bingo hall. Its progress, or decline, depending on how you look at it, is in some ways a measure of the entertainment scene in the Granite City over the years. Catholic in its tastes, Aberdeen has embraced everything from sixteenth-century Sang School psalmody to kirkyard fairgrounds, from a choir of a thousand voices to sidestreet peepshows. It has played host to world-famous musicians and conductors — and listened to Harry Gordon singing about how the girls of Fittie and Rubislaw kiss.

For a city dogged by a reputation for dourness — Lewis Grassic Gibbon said bleakness, not meanness or jollity, was the keynote to Aberdonian character — it has enjoyed itself with remarkable gusto. Perhaps it took its cue from the poet William Dunbar, who gave the townsfolk a friendly piece of advice when James IV's young Queen, Margaret Tudor, visited Aberdeen in 1511. 'Be blyth and blissful burgh of Aberdein,' he told them. Nearly five centuries later they are still paying heed to the advice.

Although he wrote *Grey Granite,* Grassic Gibbon never had much good to say about the Granite City. He should have read up on his history. He would have found the 'bleak' Aberdonian dancing round the Maypole, watching Miracle Plays at the Windmill-hill, helping to scoff 'twa tunnis of Inglis beir' at the Market Cross in celebration of James VI's first-born, following the city minstrels at a Candlemas festival at the Play-field near Woolmanhill, and dressing up in 'drag' when they went carolling and dancing at Christmas and New Year's Eve. That, of course, was in Dunbar's time, but the mould hasn't changed. The Aberdonian still enjoys himself in 'all godlie merriness'.

When Aberdonians weren't being made to laugh by the town's official jester, Jok, the fule of Aberdene, they were being encouraged to sing. From the time of Queen Margaret's visit, when she was welcomed by 'the sound of menstrallis blawing to the sky', the city council has always taken an interest in the musical life of the city. Today, the tradition is maintained, not only in local groups and societies, but in council-sponsored events like the international youth festival of music, which draws young musicians to Aberdeen from all over the world.

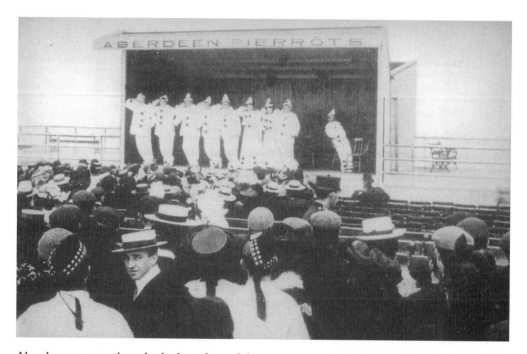

Aberdeen may not have had a brand new leisure centre to draw the crowds at the turn of the century, but it had other attractions - the Bathing for one, the Pierrots for another. 'The Pierrots, who give variety entertainments in the open air beside the Bathing Station, have proved a great attraction at the beech,' said the caption to the picture above. It first appeared in *132 Views of the Granite City*, published in 1903. Another picture showed bathing huts at the edge of the water. Even in those days, the city council was planning new developments at the beach. 'When the magnificent esplanade in course of construction towards the Don has been completed,' said one writer, 'the beach will be almost unrivalled.' Picture by courtesy of the Aberdeen Tourist Board.

It was followed a few years ago by an alternative music festival, brought about by a number of councillors who thought that the international festival was too highbrow for working-class tastes.

The highlight of the opening ceremony at the first major festival in the Music Hall was a performance by the city police pipe band — a different kind of 'blawing to the sky'. It was a reminder that the council once employed its own pipers — the 'piparis of Abirdene'. The pipers often provided a seventeenth-century version of 'Music While You Work'. In 1607, during the building of a new breakwater, labourers toiled to the strains of the town's bagpipes. But Aberdeen has never really been a piping community. In 1630, the town's piper was dismissed because a fickle public regarded his music as a public nuisance.

The council also had a fiddler and a trumpeter in its pay, as well as a flute player, John Cowpar, who acted as a kind of musical knocker-up. Aberdeen's craftsmen were wakened at four o'clock in the morning by the sound of Cowpar's German flute and the clash of a tambourine played by a servant

Deck-chairs, bathing huts, ice-cream stalls…and the golden sands black with people. I hat was Aberdeen Beach until the motor car and changing holiday habits put an end to such scenes. Up on the 'prom' are the Beach Baths, a redbrick monstrosity with towers, turrets and a tall chimney, opened in 1896, and (right) the Beach Shelter. The Baths were demolished many years ago and the Shelter met the same fate a few years ago. Picture by courtesy of Aberdeen Journals.

accompanying him. The idea was that working folk would 'pass to their labours in due and convenient time'. Cowpar made his round of the streets again at eight o'clock in the evening, presumably to knock up the night-shift. He was made redundant in 1569 when the council decided to stop playing musical alarm clocks and ring the parish kirk bell instead.

The city has produced many musical organisations. One of the first was the Aberdeen Musical Society, formed in 1748. The town's top people joined its ranks — professors, lairds, provosts, businessmen and artists — and among them was Francis Peacock, the city's dancing master, who is remembered by a yellow plaque near Peacock's Close in the Castlegate.

When the nimble-footed Mr Peacock wrote a book on the theory and practice of dancing, the town council bought twenty copies, which made a local poet put up a prayer for the councillors' safely:

> God prosper long our Lord Provost,
> Town Clerk, an' Bailies' a';
> An' grant that in their reelin' fits,
> Doup-scud *(heavily on the backside)* they winna fa'.

Mr Peacock, who was still dancing the night away when he died in 1807 at the age of eighty-four, organised the Musical Society's orchestra for the Coronation of George III in 1761. The Broadgate trembled to the blast and brrumphh of the 'drums, pipes and French horns of the Gentlemen of the Musical Society' as they led a boisterous procession down to the Market Cross in the Castlegate, where they drank the health of the King and other members of the Royal Family.

The coming of the nineteenth century brought no lessening of interest in music. William Carnie, a local journalist and poet, lectured on psalmody to an audience of 2000 and organised a 'Choir of a Thousand Voices', which packed out the Music Hall. Carnie gave the Town Council credit for its part in encouraging music in the city, but drew back from an over-ripe comment by an earlier critic that the Lord Provost and Bailies were 'a harmonious heavenly concert of as many musicians as Magistrates'.

While the well-off dressed in top hats and tails to listen to their concerts and choirs — they even held *mourning* concerts when somebody important died — ordinary mortals had largely to content themselves with the music of street musicians. They could have done worse. Some of the street musicians were highly-skilled performers. Johnnie Melven, a blind fiddler who lived in the Shiprow and had a sign above his door proclaiming his occupation, often played on steamers trading between Aberdeen and Newhaven. There were a number of 'blin' fiddlers' in the town, including Willie Milne, who played until he had raised enough money to fill his sneeshin mull (snuff-box).

The street players brought colour to the town, but they were outshone by another type of entertainer — the travelling showman. Aberdeen was besieged by itinerant showmen at the beginning of last century. They came with their peepshows and panoramas, their human and animal freaks, their two-headed boys and boneless men, plus a formidable line-up of monkeys, elephants, cockatoos, lions and other wild animals. The town folk grew fond of the performers — the four-legged ones, at anyrate — and the *Aberdeen Journal* noted with sadness the passing of 'Mr Pidcock's famous lion', which was for ten years 'the terror and admiration of thousands of visitors'. The paper added that during its last illness the lion was 'attended by seven physicians'.

The shows and exhibitions were staged on any vacant piece of ground that

Aberdeen's own comedian, Harry Gordon, once introduced a collection of mean Aberdonian stories with the lines, 'Some are fiction, some are true, some are old, few are new'. True or not, tales about tight-fisted Aberdonians have been pouring out from a mythical Aberdeen Joke Factory for the best part of this century. In 1925, a book called Canny Tales fae Aberdeen carried an illustration that must have been regarded as the ultimate insult — a view entitled 'Aberdeen on a Flag Day'. It showed Union Street completely deserted. Of course, as the book pointed out, the streets weren't always empty. Another illustration showed them packed with people — on a house-to-house collection day. Still, Aberdonians have become accustomed to 'mean Aberdonian' stories and know how to deal with them. They settle the argument over a dram, taking their line from an old Aberdeen proverb that says, 'If ony man insults ye by offerin' ye a drink — swallow the insult.' Picture by courtesy of the Aberdeen Tourist Board.

could be found. In 1816, before the building of the Union Street Facade, Polito's Menagerie, the biggest ever seen in the north up to that time, was housed in what is now part of St Nicholas Churchyard. The ground there was virtually a fairground, peopled by jugglers, knife-throwers, giants, dwarfs, and fire-eaters, until the churchyard was extended in 1819.

The panorama, forerunner of the cinema, was all the rage. In 1821, people crowded into Auchintoul's New Hall in Union Street to see the 'Bombardment of Algiers', which was shown to the accompaniment of a military band at each of its five daily performances. Away from the centre of the town, the Taits held court in George Street, at the corner of John Street, where Mrs Tait lifted a blacksmith's anvil by the hair of her head while Mr Tait did his bit by swallowing knives and forks.

In John Street itself, not far from where the new John Lewis store — the old 'Co-opy' — now stands, one travelling showman set up his caravan and introduced his wonderful blue 'oss.

'Walk up, walk up, ladies and ge'men, and see the wonderful blue 'oss,' he cried. 'This is the wonderfullest hanimal as ever was seen; 'e 'as not an 'air on all 'is body; 'e was foaled under an avalanche in Switzerland, and when 'e was found 'is mother were dead. Walk up now, you can neva 'ave such another hopotunity.'

The finest granite building on Aberdeen's Union Street- the Music Hall. The work of Archibald Simpson, it was built in 1820 as the Assembly Rooms. The project was completed by James Matthews in 1858 when the Music Hall was added to the north and in Golden Square, but the whole structure is now known as the Music Hall. The original ballroom was turned into a cloakroom and toilets in the renovations of a few years ago.

His stay in the city was a short one, for too few people took advantage of the 'hopotunity', although some people said it was because the owner of the horse was too fond of Devanha Entire, a potent product of the Devanha Brewery. At anyrate, he sold up and went on his way.

The story of the wonderful blue 'oss was told by William Buchanan in *Glimpses of Olden Days in Aberdeen*. Buchanan was glad when the freaks and wild beasts disappeared. He thought the shows were 'very dangerous places of amusement' and that 'the immorality carried on within them often led to the ruin and degradation of many'. Buchanan may have been right and no one could have regretted the disappearance of human freaks from the entertainment scene, but something was lost when that era came to an end.

When the travelling shows were in full swing, an English visitor to the town, the Revd James Hall, in a book called *Travels in Scotland*, commented on another interest of pleasure-loving Aberdonians — clubs and pubs. 'Some of them meet together like the common tradesmen of London at a public-house every night,' he said. He pointed the finger at two magistrates, Bailie Burnett

The great storm of December, 1908, left Rosemount Viaduct with several feet of snow. More than 700 men worked through the night of December 29 to clear the streets and pavements. The men, ill-clad, had to face intense cold. Some collapsed and had to be taken home. Despite the storm, some sturdy Aberdonians still went out. Here, William Wallace, looking down from his icy pedestal, seems to be drawing attention to the graceful silhouettes of women tramphing through the snow in shawls and ankle-length skiirts. Picture by courtesy of Aberdeen City Libraries.

and Bailie Littlejohn, who met in a local tavern every night of the week. 'What first failed Bailie Littlejohn was his tongue, what failed first in Bailie Burnett was his legs,' said Mr Hall, who then went on to relate how, about two or three o'clock in the morning, Bailie Littlejohn would take Bailie Burnett on his back and stagger off home.

Nowadays, although some councillors are known to have a taste for Scotland's native drink, they are more circumspect. One member, Councillor Richard (Dick) Gallagher, produced a booklet giving the names of all the city hostelries, old and new, and it was more than likely that among them was the howff where Bailie Burnett's legs went from under him. The Lemon Tree Hotel, mentioned in Dick Gallagher's book, stood in Huxter Row. It was, according to all reports, 'a quiet, cosy howff, run by 'old, couthie, courteous Mrs Ronald', who served up creamy Finnan haddocks and magnificent partan claws. There were claws of a different kind at the Lemon Tree too — Mrs

Ronald kept an eagle in a cage for many years — 'the largest and prettiest specimen I ever saw, either alive or stuffed', reported one observer. The Lemon Tree Inn disappeared when work began on the municipal buildings in 1867.

The best-known hostelry was the New Inn, which was demolished when the North of Scotland Bank (now the Archibald Simpson Restaurant) was built at the corner of King Street in 1842. It was so popular that when dames Boswell arrived there with Dr Samuel Johnson in September, 1773, he found the 'house full' sign up. He was told he could sleep in 'a little press-bed' if he shared a room with Dr Johnson. 'I had it wheeled out into the dining room,' he recorded, 'and there I lay very well.'

Robert Burns spent a night in the New Inn and George Coleman, the famous dramatist, stared out of its windows at a Highland Regiment of Fencibles 'dolefully drawn up in the drizzling rain, ankle-deep in mud'. 'The drone of a bagpipe,' said Coleman, 'kept *Maggy Laudering* and *Lochaber no moring,* enough to drive its hearers melancholy mad.'

There were more modest places in which to wine and dine in the Castlegate area. The old Poultry Market lay between Queen Street and King Street and one of the entrances was by the Maut Hillock, which got its name from the number of public houses in that corner of the market. Watty Reid was mine host at one of them. He was a bit of a wag. His howff, the haunt of tradesmen and soldiers from the Castlehill Barracks, echoed to the sound of singing well into the night. Watty had a verse painted over his fireplace:

> Fine Devanha porter; gweed strong ale;
> Real Cabrach whisky, as ever bore the bell:
> Watty's liquor's gweed; Watty's measure's just:
> Gin ye hae nae money, Watty has nae trust.

Not far away, over in the Adelphi, was Mrs Liffen's Hall, adjacent to the Adelphi Hotel, where you could enjoy 'the best native oysters from the London markets' while being entertained by people like Sam Cowell, who was described by William Carnie as 'one of the best comic singers of the day'. There were many others — Sim Reeves, just out of his teens (was he the Elvis Presley of a century ago?), Lloyd, a 'low comedian', and a character called Little Barlow, 'a dainty warbler and a master of the banjo', who brought the house down with a song about a bee buzzing around his instrument.

Some people got a bee in their bonnet about W. G. Ross, a baritone, who, according to Carnie, created a sensation in London with a song called 'Sam Hall', which was supposed to be the outpourings of a criminal the night before his execution. Ross never inflicted this 'repulsive composition' on the delicate ears of Mrs Liffen's guests, but he apparently did respond to requests to sing it in another 'well-frequented hostelry'. Perhaps it was Watty Reid's customers who stamped and shouted for 'Sam Hall'. Mr Carnie was in the audience —

A view that changed dramatically after buildings on the south side of Upperkirkgate were demolished in the 1950s to allow widening of the street. The block on the north side of Schoolhill was built after the demolition of George Jamesone's house in 1886 so that Wordie and Company, railway agents and carriers, could expand their premises. Now even more sweeping changes have taken place, with St Nicholas Street and George Street blocked off by new shopping malls. Picture by courtesy of Aberdeen City Libraries.

strictly for professional reasons, of course. 'It was not,' he said primly, 'a wholesome exhibition.'

The ghosts of Sim Reeves and Little Barlow sigh around the once-elegant Adelphi. There is nothing to show that Mrs Liffen's establishment ever existed, and the names of the artistes who sang and danced while customers gobbled down their London oysters are long forgotten. In the eighteen-fifties and sixties the city was awash with entertainers. Playhouses and music halls sprang up everywhere. There was a playhouse in shabby little Shoe Lane, which was virtually wiped out by developments in Queen Street, and another called 'Coachy's Playhouse' (its owner was a coach proprietor) in nearby Chronicle Lane, while a third operated in a Queen Street inn. The Alhambra in Exchange Street was a popular theatre. The Town Council even got in on the act. Shortly after the building of the Music Hall, the Lord Provost, Sir Alexander Anderson, called a meeting of leading citizens to promote Saturday Evening Concerts.

The Music Hall concerts cost you anything from 2d to 2s, but in less stylish halls it was even cheaper. Some of them, like the Penny Rattler in Bool Road, were the nineteenth-century equivalent of the cinema flea pits that sprang up early this century, but a lot less respectable. The Bool or Bowl Road, originally Albion Street, ran down to the Links. It was said to be 'a haunt of dissipation' and 'a hot-bed of vice', while the Bool Road Theatre (the Penny Rattler) was condemned as a 'den of iniquity'. 'Scottie's Show' in John Street, home of the famous blue 'oss, was another place where you could pay a penny for an evening of drama, dancing and singing.

The famous Wizard of the North, John Henry Anderson, started his career at Scottie's. He was Scottie's right-hand man (he eventually married his daughter) and it was Scottie who taught him one of his first tricks, 'the great gun trick'. He started up on his own as an illusionist in the 1830s and worked for almost forty years before dying in England in 1874. He once amazed Queen Victoria at Balmoral by producing out of the air hats, bird cages, a live goose, goldfish in bowls, and his own son Oscar in full Highland dress.

Anderson, who called himself 'Professor', was the Paul Daniels of his time, a clever illusionist, but in that more superstitious age some people regarded the self-styled Wizard as Aul' Nick himself. One of his landladies, coming upon his umbrella with 'The Wizard of the North' inscribed on it, said she could smell the brimstone on him. She told him to go, handing him back the four half-crowns he had paid in advance. 'The de'il's in my pouch dancing wi' the half-croons,' she declared.

The Wizard of the North went out with a ghoulish flourish. His coffin had an open glass-covered square through which the corpse's face could be seen. He is buried in St Nicholas Churchyard beside his mother, Mary Robertson, whose headstone carries the lines:

> Yes! she had friends when fortune smiled;
> It frowned, they knew her not;
> She died; the orphans wept, but lived
> To mark this hallowed spot.

No one knows what story lay behind this bitter little verse. Below it is the inscription, 'John H. Anderson, Wizard of the North, died February 3rd, 1874, aged 60 years.'

Down in busy Virginia Street an archway opens on to a small close with the name Theatre Lane. This was at one time the rear entrance to the Theatre Royal in Marischal Street, the city's first permanent theatre, known as the Old Band Box. The Wizard of the North graduated from Scottie's to the Theatre Royal, which was opened in 1795. It was not the most handsome theatre in the town; one visitor said it looked as if it had been made out of old orange boxes and ruined market stalls. Unruly patrons threw orange peel at each other

The Bon-Accord coat-of-arms in Union Terrace Gardens. This corner of the gardens is used each year for a special floral display. Behind are His Majesty's Theatre and St Mark's Church. The future of Union Terrace Gardens has been debated at length in recent years; one suggestion, hotly opposed, was that it should be covered over and turned into a car park.

and chucked mutton pies into the pit, and an army of bootless feet stamped a demand for 'Music! Music!' Nevertheless, it hosted some big-name performers.

Aberdeen audiences are said to be hard to please. That was certainly the case a century ago. In September, 1888, a new hall, known as the Bon-Accord Music Hall, opened in St Nicholas Lane. Magistrates and councillors turned up at the opening ceremony to talk grandly about the great era of theatre that lay ahead. Leading lady artistes were presented with beautiful bouquets. All seemed set for success. Not long after, however, the theatre was completely wrecked by a dissatisfied audience. It never re-opened. The foot-stamping pie-throwers of the Old Band box and the mindless wreckers of the Bon-Accord Music Hall are a reminder that hooliganism is not just a present-day problem.

Despite this setback, the turn of the century brought important changes in the Aberdeen entertainment scene. The Theatre Royal closed in 1872, but its place was taken by Her Majesty's Opera House in Guild Street, which opened the same year. It later became Her Majesty's Theatre, surviving under that name until His Majesty's Theatre opened in 1906.

In 1891 the Jollity Vaudeville Theatre was launched. It shut its doors two years later, but close on its heels came the People's Palace, which was to carry the theatrical tradition well into the twentieth century before (under another name) it took Aberdeen audiences into the cinema age. Many of the great names of music hall trod the boards at the Palace. Harry Lauder was there in his early days, and splashed across the billboards were names like Florrie Ford and Harry Tate, Dan Leno and Bransby Williams, Charles Coburn and Walford Bodie, and it is thought that a youngster called Charlie Chaplin once appeared there. Hackenshchmidt the wrestler and Mahmout the Terrible Turk were also among the stars.

There was a cinematograph at the Palace as early as 1902, but it was not until 1931, when it was bought by Jack Poole, that it became a picture house. The Pooles was one of a number of cinemas whose names were to become as familiar to Aberdonians as Union Street itself. Many of them were built on or near the city's main street...the unassuming little Belmont Cinema in Belmont Street; the Cinema House, just round the corner from Union Terrace; the Playhouse at the west end of Union Street, with its long marble stairway leading to the main foyer; the Kingsway in King Street.

The Donald empire had its roots in the cinema industry. James F. Donald literally took his first steps in the entertainment world by starting up a dancing class — the Gondolier Quadrille Party — in a hall in Huntly Street in 1891, later moving to North Silver Street, but the silver screen beckoned him. He opened a cinema in a former billiard hall at 475 Union Street, and because it was above the premises of the Aberdeen Dairy it was quickly dubbed 'The Tuppenny Freezer'. In 1935, *David Copperfield* played to packed houses in the Granite City. It was billed as 'The Picture that is too Big for one Theatre' — and it was screened at both the Capitol and Playhouse.

Aberdeen was cinema-daft. Going to the pictures was a firmly-ingrained habit of pre-war years, and in 1939 the city had no fewer than nineteen cinemas. The decline began in the 1960s, but even in this television-besotted age the lure of the cinema is still strong. Who knows, a new generation, untutored in cinema lore, may one day see the bingo halls shout their last 'House!' and revert to the magic world of 'the flicks'.

Despite their enthusiasm for the cinema, Aberdeen audiences stayed loyal, and still do, to the stage. In 1910, Her Majesty's Theatre in Guild Street reopened as the Tivoli. One of its first performers was a juggler who was later to become well-known as a film actor. He took the part of Mr Micawber in *David Copperfield,* the film that was too big for one theatre. He had a bulbous nose, a nasal accent, and curious views on children and dogs — anyone who disliked them, he said, couldn't be all that bad. His name was W.C. Fields.

But it was as the home of a generation of Scots comedians that the Tivoli was to make its name, men like Dave Willis, Will Fyffe, Johnny Beattie, Jimmy Logan, and a host of others. Among them was a local loon, born in 1892, who was to laugh, joke and sing his way into the hearts of Aberdeen theatregoers. His full name was Alexander Ross Gordon, but to everyone who saw him at the Tivoli in the early 1930s, or at the Beach Pavilion and His Majesty's Theatre, he was known simply as Harry Gordon, the Laird of Inversnecky.

Some people believed that there really *was* a place called Inversnecky, others thought it was the Beach Pavilion, but Harry, in one of his sketches, put it outside Aberdeen. It was a bit like the mythical Auchterturra of 'Scotland the What?' fame. When people asked where it was, Buff Hardy and his colleagues reeled off a list of North-east villages — Maud, Methlick, Udny, Rhynie, Fogie, and so on — and then said it wasn't any of them. But, they added, it *could* be one of them. Inversnecky had 'a picture hoose and public hoose', a Doctor, a Lamplighter, a Beadle, and a Barber who was liable to 'cut a bittie aff a mannie's nose'.

Not so long ago I heard an old '78' record by Harry Gordon. The needle scraped away the years as the Laid of Inversnecky's unmistakable Aberdeen voice began to sing 'I wish I was Single Again' — 'When I took a wife I was sentenced for life, Oh, I wish I was single again.' On the other side was 'A Song of Cove'. Harry thought Cove was far enough to go for a holiday — 'I've nae eese for places faur ye canna get a dram.' If he wanted a change of air he knew where to get it:

> I tak my bike tae Cove,
> Tak my bike tae Cove,
> Faur the air is as strong as can be,
> For ye only need one guff
> Tae feel ye've had enough
> By the side of the silvery sea.

The song was written in the days when Cove, on the outskirts of Aberdeen, was just about as far as working people could hope to get on their holidays. The lyrics would never have won any awards; they were by A.F. Hyslop, an Inspector of Schools, who wrote under the name of Forbes Hazelwood. If they were crude, it didn't matter. Harry used them to put himself over as a typical Aberdonian and he struck a chord with his audiences.

The fact that he himself was an Aberdonian didn't prevent him from cashing in on the vogue for mean Aberdonian stories (after all, Aberdeen invented them) and he had a fund of them — that Aberdeen motorists took every corner on two wheels to save wear on the tyres, that Scotsmen were fond of rubber because it gave, and that an Aberdonian never finished his soup because he hated to tip the plate. One of his Granite City stories was about a man who went for a haircut:

The North Church in King Street was once called the Pepperpot Kirk by Aberdonians because of its distinctive tower. Architectural purists probably shuddered at the description, for the tower's design was based on a structure in Athens known as the Choragic Monument of Lysicrates — the Tower of the Winds. This Grecian-style building, which was the first of John Smith's classical designs, was built in 1829–30. Now longer a kirk, it became the Aberdeen Arts Centre, but in 1998 there were moves to close it.

Customer — 'Fit dae ye charge for a haircut?'
Barber — 'Eightpence.'
Customer — 'And foo muckle for a shave?'
Barber — 'Fourpence.'
Customer — 'Weel, gie ma heid a shave.'

He sang about things that were familiar to his listeners, about 'fowk fae Constitution Street an' fowk fae Rubislaw Den'. He often tilted at the notes and snobs in the Elysian suburbs of Rubislaw. In a song called 'How our Girls Kiss' he said that the Ferryhill girls grabbed their men like terriers, but the Rubislaw girls bowed their stately heads and let their boyfriends sip. He was the champion of the downtrodden husband:

'Hoo are ye gettin' on wi' the wife?'
'Fine. We're nae speakin'.'

Harry Gordon wasn't the first local comedian to make a name for himself, but nobody else reached quite the same heights. He first appeared at His Majesty's Theatre in 1923 and was still going strong with his 'Five-Past Eight' shows well into the post-war years. At the Braemar Gathering in 1950 he was presented to King George VI, but, unlike the Laird of Lauder Ha', he never became Sir Harry. There were a lot of people who thought he should have.

Doric comedy hasn't changed much since an entertainer called Dufton Scott, from Inverurie, set out to capture North-east audiences sixty years ago. The 'Scotland the What?' team have Auchterturra and Sandy Thomson, who is usually found asking the Rhynie telephone operator, 'Is that you, Beldie?' Dufton Scott, on the other hand, had Blowieneuck and Sandy Macsiccar. When the lad from Blowieneuk came to the Music Hall to hear Sousa, he got so carried away that he found himself stamping briskly to the music — on his neighbour's feet. 'I had been duntin' awe wi' my big tackety beets on the puir craiter's taes a' the time! I was richt putten oot, an' I says — 'I'm verra sorry, lassie; I didna ken I was touchin' ye. Are ye bother't muckle wi' corns?' It could have come straight from a 'Scotland the What?' script.

Another entertainer with a large following was Rab the Rhymer, who in real life was Dr Douglas S. Raitt, a scientist with the Scottish Fisheries Research Department at Aberdeen. He wrote, sang and broadcast his own songs, and for many years his identity was kept a secret. In 1938 he was looking ahead and wondering what things would be like in 1988:

The experts for eence a' agree
That a dwindlin' nation are we,
And in nineteen hunder en' echty-echt
I winder fit Britain will dee.

The 'Scotland the What' team — Butt Hardie, Steve Robertson and George Donald outside their spiritual home, His Majesty's Theatre. There was a fourth member of the team, the late Jimmy Logan, who was producer. They took their show to 'foreign' places like Glasgow and Edinburgh, but they were at their best in front of the Aberdeen audiences whose lives, loves and language they mirrored with gentle mocking honesty. Picture by courtesy of the Aberdeen Tourist Board.

He was never to find out. He was killed in an accident outside his home in Angus in 1944 at the age of forty-two. During his time at Aberdeen University, Douglas Raitt wrote 'Town and Gown', the students' gala week show at HM Theatre. The format has changed little over the years, and it is one on which 'Scotland the What?' built its success.

The 'Scotland the What?' team — Buff Hardie, Steve Robertson, George Donald, and producer Jimmy Logan — were the natural inheritors of the Gordon-Raitt tradition, but there was a change of emphasis. There were no props. There were no tartan tammies. They appeared in evening suits, which sometimes sats oddly with a broad Aberdeen tongue relating how 'me an' some o' the boys wis haein' a drink last nicht in *The Glaikit Stirk*'. They had an obsession with Clatt. Sandy Thomson's brother Willie worked at Rhynie and lived at Clatt. 'Maist nichts fan he gings hame, even *he* canna find Clatt.' It is a situation that seemed likely to change, for 'Scotland the What?' had put Clatt on the map.

Sandy Thomson may be a mythical figure, but some of the characters are real enough. Like Frank Lefevre, a shrewd city solicitor, who is seen by the public as having the kind of image usually reserved for hard-hitting American laywers on TV. 'Far's Frunkie Lefevre the day? Oh, he's a great Frunkie, is he? He's a great Frunkie! Frunkie selt my hoose for me. Took a bit o' daein, it was a coonicil hoose.' Lefevre stirred up a legal hornet's nest by starting up a 'no win, no fee' American-style compensation service. It is a safe bet that Frunkie's latest ploy would end up on the 'Scotland the What?' stage.

The show's title and its mocking philosophy was explained in the lines from one of their songs:

> Pope John Paul the Second
> Is a Rangers fan,
> Sylvester Stallone is gay
> And Dolly Parton is a man.
> But the strangest reputation
> Is the one that Scotland's got:
> When folk sing *Scotland the Brave,*
> We say 'Scotland the What?'

The lines of the song were changed when they went on what Buff Hardie described to me as their 'foreign tour' to alien places like Glasgow and Edinburgh, but, unlike other Scots entertainers, they never went in for annual pilgrimages abroad. They have, however, considered it. Jimmy Logan once told me they were thinking about going overseas, but later, giving me his quizzical STW look, Buff remarked: 'We've aye been threatenin' that!'

Their spiritual home was His Majesty's Theatre. This theatre, which was taken over by the Donald family in 1933, has run the gamut of entertainment in the past half-century, from Shakespearian drama to music hall comedy, from ballet and opera to panto and local amateur shows — and even an occasional dip into the world of the cinema. Aberdeen Town Council bought it from the Donalds in 1973 to prevent a takeover by Ladbrokes, but there was still a Donald at its head — Jimmy Donald, grandson of the man who took it over fifty-six years ago.

Jimmy Donald, who was retained to manage the theatre, had inherited the family trait of staying out of the limelight and getting on with the job, but under him 'His Majesty's' went from strength to strength. Rab the Rhymer wondered what lay ahead in nineteen hunder an' echty-echt. Well, as they say, we ken noo. What lies ahead in two thousand and echty-echt is another matter; no one can see that far ahead. But it is probably safe to say that by the end of this century HM Theatre will still be flourishing, and that, perhaps, a familiar voice from the stage will be heard asking, in a broad Aberdeen accent, 'Is that you, Beldie?'

CHAPTER SEVEN
Bobbies and Batons

A walk in the woods of Thainstone, near Inverurie, on Saturday 3 December, 1864, ended in the brutal murder of a 52-year-old Aberdeen woman, Mrs Ann Forbes, wife of a Virginia Street shoemaker. That day, Mrs Forbes travelled fourteen miles from Aberdeen to Thainstone to meet the man who had been her lover for a number of years. He was George Stephen, a 62-year-old Port Elphinstone wood merchant, and his affair with Mrs Forbes was no secret in this quiet corner of the Garioch. They had often been seen together strolling in the woods. This time, however, there was a difference — Stephen was carrying an axe.

He was seen some time later, still carrying the axe, and between two and three in the afternoon a boy came upon the body of a woman lying among the trees. It was Mrs Forbes. She was dressed in a shabby gown and a shawl, with a red flannel cloth on her head, and there was a great wound in the back of her head. She was still breathing, but she died without saying a word. Stephen was arrested and charged with murder. He denied all knowledge of it, but the following day police searched his house and found two axes, one with traces of a red substance on its 'pow'.

When he appeared at the Circuit Court in Aberdeen in the Spring of 1865 he created a sensation by pleading guilty. He was sentenced to be hanged, but the sentence was commuted at the last minute and he was ordered to be detained in an asylum at Perth Prison. He was asked if he knew what that meant. 'Oh, aye,' he replied, 'jist a whilie langer tae live.'

The axe with the blood on its 'pow' is still in the hands of the police — the oldest exhibit in the North-east's first Black Museum, or, to give it its official name, the Grampian Police Heritage Museum. Police lamps, bobbies' bicycles, batons, photographs, a birch, old documents, a sharp-edged shovel which a woman used to commit suicide in a coal cellar, and a bootlace used in a strangulation case — these have all found their way into the police museum. But the ugliest exhibit is the long, heavy axe which cleaved the skull of Ann Forbes as she walked in the woods of Thainston with a lover who had murder in his heart.

The Forbes killing has long since been forgotten, but it found a place in the *Black Kalendar of Aberdeen*, a gory catalogue of crime which covers the years from 1746 to 1878 and contains everything from a report on how a mother killed her child by dashing its head against the stone wall of a pig-sty (she pleaded guilty to a minor charge of concealing a pregnancy and was sent to prison for twelve months) to accounts of criminals singing psalms on the scaffold before they were executed. People were sentenced to transportation for seven or ten years for comparatively minor offences, and some were whipped through the streets of Aberdeen and banished for life.

James Miller, a thief who had been whipped and ordered out of the town in 1753, broke into a house at Inverurie before leaving Aberdeen and was sentenced to be hanged. He begged the judges to give him light so that he could read the Bible in the short time he had left. His body was cut down after the execution, put into a coffin, and taken to the Gallowhills to be collected for dissection. To save him from the surgeon's knife a group of sympathetic sailors carried him off, sailed out of the port in a yawl, and sank the body in the sea.

The year 1849 was a bad year for crime in Aberdeen. The Autumn Circuit court, according to the *Black Kalendar*, highlighted 'such a fearful amount of atrocity as to render the task of recording the trials a painful duty'. But in those bad old days the punishment was almost as terrible as the crime, for our forefathers were ruthless in their determination to uphold law and order.

One example is the case of a man called James Aberdein, who cut down a young birch tree at Hilton. There is no record of why he did it — perhaps he wanted some kindling for his fire — but today, for that sort of offence, he would probably be given a small fine. Aberdein, however, lived in the middle of the eighteenth century, and what he got was four months in the Tolbooth. That wasn't all. He was ordered to be 'publicly whipped through the town of Aberdeen upon the last Friday of each of the said four months between the hours of twelve and two'.

There used to be a quaint old custom of presenting a pair of white gloves to Aberdeen magistrates if no cases came before the court. The same sort of practice was followed in Circuit courts, but there were usually so many cases in the senior courts that the glove ceremony was seldom observed. The Spring and Autumn Circuits in 1781 were exceptions, as was one of the Circuit Courts in 1781. On this occasion the judge was Lord Braxfield, who was said to be a coarse and unfeeling man. When Braxfield got his white gloves one writer remarked that he was probably disappointed — to him 'the sentencing of a poor wretch to the gallows seemed rather a pleasure than a disagreeable duty'.

Nor could anyone turn to the Kirk for compassion. The clerical Braxfields who appeared after the Reformation were bigoted and intolerant. In 1562, when the church session of Aberdeen was constituted, fourteen lay elders and seven deacons, led by the chief magistrate of the town, enforced the Kirk's decrees. The kirk session had all the authority of a court of law. It guarded the morals of the people by whipping, ducking, banishing, excommunication, fining, or imprisoning offenders in the vaults of the kirks. The Church put a good deal of stress on family discipline. The use of the strap was encouraged. It was called a palmer, which was no doubt the origin of the modern 'palmies' and 'pandies', handed out in schools before the abolition of corporal punishment. Swearing, filthy speaking, or 'uncomely behaviour in any families' had to be 'sharply punished with a palmer on the hand'. 'For keiping of guid order within families of Aberdene' the church session laid down that there should be a palmer in every house. The master of the house was given the job of administering it, not only to his family but to servants.

The sumptuary laws of that time, laws regulating conduct in religious and moral matters, told people what to eat and drink, what to wear, and what to avoid — playing cards or dice, for instance. They were even told the time to go to bed at night and the time to get up in the morning, one by the curfew bell and the other by a band of musicians or minstrels going through the streets.

People who spread malicious rumours about their neighbours were put in the cock or cuckstool and had to publicly proclaim, 'Tongue, ye lied'. The cuckstool was used in Aberdeen as far back as the fourteenth century. Cuck or cock is a corruption of the Gaelic word *cnoc*, a hill, which indicates that the long beam used in the stool rested on a hillock. This seesaw, which also turned round in any direction, had a small chair fixed to one end. The prisoner was tied into it and the man in charge, holding a rope attached to the other end, pulled it up and down so that the victim was dipped into water. A refinement of this was the Cran in James Street, near Weigh-house Square. The Cran loaded and unloaded ships in the harbour, but was also used for the public ducking of 'adulterers, fornicators and whoremongers'.

In July, 1638, ducking at the Cran was part of the punishment for Jeills Paterson when she admitted fornicating with an Adam Down on board a ship in the harbour. After the ducking, she was ordered to be confined in the correction-house till the following Whitsunday — and whipped every Monday during that period. Fornication was a sin that brought heavy penalties from the kirk session. Another woman, Elspet Taylor, who committed adultery with an Alex Robertson in 1640, was scourged at the mercat cross, carted through the streets with a paper crown on her head, and publicly banished from the town.

The ritual of carting harlots, whores and adulterers through the streets with paper hats on their heads was intended as a public humiliation, as well as serving as a warning to anybody with wandering eyes and wicked thoughts, but it also provided 'entertainment' for the masses. Hanging was the star attraction. Hundreds of people gathered at the gibbet in front of the old Town House to watch the condemned go to their deaths looking down Marischal Street. The majority of them were women, and in October, 1830, they saw

The Mannie o' the Well looks across Castle Street to the centre of law and order in the Granite City — the old Tolbooth spire and the entrance to Lodge Walk. The Tolbooth, now incorporated behind the granite frontage of the 1868-74 Town House and Sheriff Courthouse, dates mainly from 1615 and 1627. The Granite City has had three tolbooths, the earliest dating back to the 12th century. The grim cells were known as the Mids o' Mar. These dark dungeons were reached by narrow spiral stairs and lit by small barred windows. Behind the heavy iron doors and iron yetts (gates) the prisoners were held by shackles and chains. Lodge Walk originally ran between Queen Street and Castle Street, but, with the building of modern offices for Grampian Police, only a small section remains. It took its name from the Aberdeen Lodge of Free Masons, who had premises there.

one of their own go to the gallows — the first time for forty years that a woman was publicly hanged in the city.

Her name was Catherine Davidson. She ran a public house with her husband, a butcher to trade, but there was no love lost between them. The woman had often threatened openly to cut his throat or poison him. The husband, who had forecast that one day she would 'die looking down Marischal Street', became ill and died. His wife was charged with his murder and a servant told in court how he had groaned, 'I'm burned…I'm gone…I'm roasted', and had said to his wife, 'Oh, woman, woman, you have tried to do this often and you have done it now'. She was found guilty, and after the trial she admitted that she had poured oil of vitriol down his throat while he slept — with his mouth open.

Poisoning seems to have been a favourite way of ending domestic differences. In May, 1849, James Burnett was hanged for poisoning his wife. The *Black Kalendar* reported that twelve thousand people turned up for his execution, but other accounts put it at hundreds, not thousands. On the morning of his execution, Burnett had bread and tea for breakfast, and asked to join in the singing of the hymn, 'The hour of my departure's come'. He went to the scaffold wearing a black suit and a white night-cap and his last words were, 'Lord, have mercy on my soul!'

More than a century later, another Burnett went to the scaffold — the last man to be hanged in Aberdeen. On May 31, 1963, in a house in Jackson Terrace, off King Street, Henry John Burnett, an Aberdeen labourer, shot and killed the merchant seaman husband of the woman he had been living with. Then he held up a motorist, stole his car, and fled from the city. He didn't get far. He was arrested by police at Ellon, sixteen miles from Aberdeen, and at the High Court of Justiciary in July he was found guilty of capital murder and sentenced to death.

Burnett was hanged at Craiginches Prison on August 15. It was the first death sentence to be carried out in Aberdeen for 100 years. A crowd of over 200 men and women stood in silence outside the prison. There were no scenes among the crowd, but when a number of warders left the prison at 8.15 am, fourteen minutes after the execution, there were boos and a cry of 'You murderers!' The only demonstrator was an ice-cream salesman who wore placards saying 'Abolish Legal Murder' and 'Vengeance is Mine Sayeth the Lord'.

That night the *Evening Express* carried an editorial headed A DARK SILENT DAY. The paper pointed out that the public had failed to show its feelings. Even in the days before the execution there had been 'an appalling silence from the great majority of local people'. Two years later, capital punishment was abolished. Today, the only reminder of that 'dark silent day' is a cartridge belt in the Black Museum collection. It was worn round Burnett's waist when he set out to kill his lover's husband.

Craiginches Prison, where Burnett died, perches on a hill in Torry overlooking the River Dee. Granite-built and gloomy, it was opened in 1891 to replace what was known as the East Prison in Lodge Walk. The East Prison was pulled down in 1864 and the prisoners were temporarily housed in the old County jail. From there they were taken to Craiginches in 'a bus with blinded windows, on which the prison warders mounted guard'. There were forty-three of them, and the *Aberdeen Journal* reported that they looked upon the 'flitting' as 'an agreeable break in their prison life'.

Aberdeen's first prison was in the Castlegate, which has always been the focal point of justice in the city. This was the Tolbooth, or, rather, the High Tolbooth, for there was also the Laigh Tolbooth, which was the Council Chamber. The East Prison was erected behind the Tolbooth when a new Court House was built in 1819. The year 1636 saw the building of a House of Correction, which gave its name to Correction Wynd.

The House of Correction was for vagabonds, beggars, leud leivars (lewd livers) and incorrigible harlots. Nagging wives — 'common scolds' — were also sent there, and children disobedient to parents. For the most part they were people 'not amending to the discipline of the kirk', and, taking into account the whippings and duckings handed out by the clergy, they must have been hardened cases. Another candidate for the House of Correction was the 'pyiker' (pilferer), a word still heard in Aberdeen today when someone hurls the insult 'Awe' ye piker!' The inmates had to be 'strong in body and able to work', for they were kept busy making broadcloths and kerseys (coarse woollen cloth).

The prison that claimed the title of Aberdeen's ugliest building was the Bridewell, a Bastille-like House of Correction in Rose Street. Rose Street was half the length it is now, turned into a cul-de-sac by the Bridewell's huge gateway. On the north side of the prison was Henry Street, named after Provost George Henry, whose main claim to fame seems to have been that he was the last Aberdonian to wear hair powder. The Bridewell, with its battlemented towers five storeys high, was later called the West Prison. It was demolished in 1868, although its gateway stood until 1883, when it was removed to allow Rose Street to link up with Skene Street and Esslemont Avenue.

The Bridewell and the House of Correction have gone, and there are fewer vagabonds and beggars, but the city still has its quota of 'leud leivars' and incorrigible harlots. Kerb-crawlers alarm the folk of Fittie, 'mugging' rears its ugly head, and drunks bring police patrols out on a Saturday night, but the 'sin city' image which Aberdeen occasionally shoulders as the price of being an oil town pales into insignificance against the statistics of a century ago.

In 1857 it was estimated that there were some 400 prostitutes and thirty-four brothels in the city. In time, the police were given greater powers to deal with the situation and by 1864 the number of street walkers had dropped to 180. The number of brothels had also fallen to twenty-seven. As for

Horse transport is still in use at Hazlehead Park. Here, a pair of Clydesdales pulls one of the park carts as it sets out on its rounds.

A corner shop in Aberdeen's Queen's Road which was once a toll-house.

This statue in the Hazlehead rose gardens was raised in memory of the men who lost their lives in the Piper Alpha disaster.

This striking gateway on Old Aberdeen's High Street leads to New King's, which was designed in 1912.

The kirkyard at St Fittick's Church at Nigg, which was at one time raided by body-snatchers.

King's College Chapel, Old Aberdeen.

The ancient Town House in the High Street, Old Aberdeen.

The twin spires of St Machar's Cathedral can be seen beyond this entrance.

An old pack bridge, once on the main route into Aberdeen, still stands in Ruthrieston, near the Bridge of Dee.

The new dual carriageway in the Denburn. The Triple Kirks spire can be seen in the background.

Strolling on the Prom at Aberdeen. In the background is the Beach Ballroom.

The Mercat Cross of Aberdeen stands in the shadows below the Salvation Army Citadel in the Castlegate.

This gaily-decorated shed in the fishing village of Fittie is one of a number of old fishing bothies that have been restored and put to a new use.

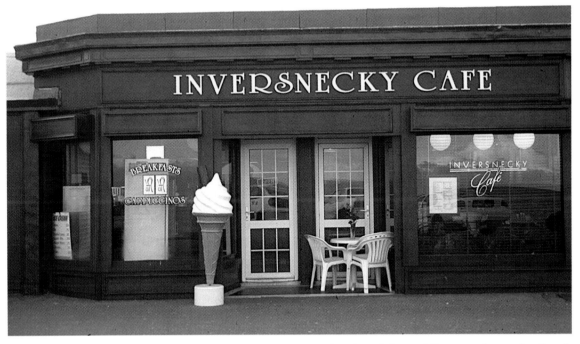

The Inversnecky Cafe at Aberdeen Beach. It stands near the site of the real Inversnecky — the Beach Pavilion — where Harry Gordon once played to packed houses.

A 'Cocky Hunter's' sign above the entrance to a bar in Union Street. It is named after the man who was king of the second-hand furniture trade in Aberdeen.

The Duke of Gordon stands guard over the crush of vehicles in the car park in Golden Square.

The statue of Prince Albert in Union Terrace. Behind it to the right is the Wallace Statue, while in the background is HM Theatre.

drunkenness, Aberdeen had a 'mobile' patrol dealing with drunks as far back as 1830. The mobility was provided by a handcart, which for over thirty years carried drunks off to the Watch-house. By 1863 it was reported to be 'completely worn out'.

Pocket-picking was rife in the middle of last century. Many East-end thieves taught youngsters how to pick pockets and then sent them out to work for them. Leading the field was a female Fagin called Annie Macdonald, who lived in a hovel in Peacock's Close and had a gang of young boys under her. She housed them, fed them, and trained them to steal, but the law caught up with her and she was sentenced to seven years' transportation.

There are some things that haven't changed. Graffiti was a problem a long time ago. When Orders and Instructions for Constables were drawn up in 1657 it was laid down that 'no improper or indecent words be written on the walls or doors'. Closing time in pubs was 'nyne acclock at nicht', and anyone haunting taverns or ale houses after that was arrested.

Policemen had to ensure that nobody chucked snowballs or made slides. They took the instruction seriously, for Alexander Clark, a Rosemount 'bobby' who wrote *Reminiscences of a Police Officer,* recalled being ordered to make a raid after complaints about boys sliding on the Hangman's Brae at Castle Street. They collared a number of youngsters, but on the way back to their office were attacked by the boys' mothers. In the end, they let the boys go and grabbed 'four of the most outrageous of the viragos'. Their howling, said Clark, was indescribable, but they were freed when their husbands turned up.

The first 'bobbies' were the Town Sergeants — the Toun's Guards — who acted as a Day Patrol. Today, their role is a more passive one, including attendance on the Lord Provost at official functions. The Night Watch took over after dark. The Watchmen wore top coats and Tam o' Shanter bonnets and carried cudgels. They were regarded as inferior to the Town Sergeants and were nicknamed 'Charlies'. The dictionary definition of a Charlie is 'a silly person', and the word is still used today in a derogatory sense.

One of the early Town Sergeants *was* a Charlie — Charlie Clapperton — but there was nothing silly about this Town House 'redcoat'. He must have had a sense of humour for he was always accompanied by a dog called 'Help', which must have created problems when he shouted on it. He built up such a reputation that his successor, Simon Grant, was at first known as 'young Clapperton'. Grant had no need to bask in Charlie's reflected glory, for he himself became the city's most famous thief-catcher. He was said to be the terror of evildoers for over half a century and he was often asked to help with cases outside the town. He lived to the age of seventy-five and was given a public funeral.

When the Burgh Reform Act was passed it was thought that town sergeants and town drummers would no longer be required and a Lament was written by one of the Town House clerks:

In the year eighteen hundred and thirty-three
A very great change in this house is to be;
The clerks, town-serjeants, town's drummers and all,
Must speedily out of its door 'tak' their crawl'.

Nothing happened — nobody 'took their crawl'. The Town Sergeants are still there today, resplendent in the red coats which were first worn by their civic predecessors in 1615. As the years marched on, the police produced officers of a calibre to equal Charlie Clapperton and Simon Grant. In those days brawn, not brain, was what made a good 'bobby'. One man who rose through the ranks from night watchman to superintendent was known as Muckle Watson because of his size, and a lofty first lieutenant called George Dey was nicknamed 'The Longest Dey'.

Grampian Police is today a force geared to scientific and technical aids that would have seemed like fantasy in the days of Simon Grant and Muckle Watson. Aberdeen's first 'Chief Constable' was appointed in 1880. He was Superintendent Thomas Wyness, a Midmar man, who joined the Aberdeen-shire Constabulary as a constable in 1859 and served at Elgin and Inverness before being appointed Superintendent, the 'Chief's' rank, at Aberdeen. He was a strong-willed character who was held in awe by the magistrates. A poem called 'A Prayer' suggested that 'the six Temperance Bailies' of Aberdeen should be taken to Heaven because they were too good for Bon-Accord, and that a place might be found for Number Seven —

Superintendent Wyness:

Ye're sure ye hae nae vacant place
For this chief, Number Seven?
Oh Lord, we tell ye tae yer face,
He maun get intae Heaven!
And there he must be King alone
An Autocratic Highness,
Come doon yersel' free Heaven's Throne,
An' han' the reins tae Wyness!

Towards the close of the nineteenth century Aberdeen was shocked by a crime that revived memories of the Burkin' Hoose sensation of 1831. This was the Nellfield Cemetery Scandal of 1899, in which the cemetery superintendent, William Coutts, was arrested and charged with six violations of graves at Nellfield.

Coffins had been removed and burned, bodies disinterred and buried elsewhere, corpses thrown into graves and covered by coffin lids after the coffins had been burned, other bodies trailed from one grave to another, and at least one body broken up with a shovel. The ghoulish plan behind all this was to create more space, which was then sold for new interments. After a four-day trial, Coutts pleaded guilty to two of the charges of violating sepulchres and was sent to jail for six months.

Nearly half a century later the Granite City faced yet another burial scandal, but this time the setting was the Aberdeen Crematorium at Kaimhill. The Coffin Lids Case of 1944 created so much feeling that the trial was held in Edinburgh. The men in the dock were a town councillor called James Dewar, who was managing director of the Crematorium, and Alick George Forbes, a local undertaker. In the Nellfield Cemetery Scandal unrelated bodies were buried together to create more interment space; in the Crematorium case unrelated bodies were cremated together after coffin lids had been removed.

The war-time shortage of wood lay behind this grisly action. Wood from coffin lids and coffins was used by Crematorium workers and others to make wireless cabinets, tea trays, a bureau — and black-out shutters! Dewar was found guilty of the theft of one thousand and forty coffin lids and two coffins. He was sent to jail for three years. Forbes was convicted of the reset of one hundred coffin lids and imprisoned for six months.

The cudgels of the Watchmen became the batons of the 'Bobbies' when a fish war broke out in Aberdeen in April 1923. The use of the police in trade-union disputes has been fiercely debated in comparatively recent years, particularly during the miners' strike and the Wapping newspaper confrontation, but there was no dubiety about the police role when Aberdeen fishermen went on strike some sixty-five years ago. Their strike was in protest at the landing of German-caught fish at the port. The police were called in when the strikers stopped porters from entering the Fish Market to unload one vessel.

One porter and a police inspector were assaulted and the police drew their batons and charged the strikers, clearing the Market. The following morning, about 3000 strikers gathered at Point Law, marched to the Fish Market, and took control of it. They cast four German trawlers adrift and bombarded the crews with fish and lumps of ice. Eighty policemen were sent in. They charged the strikers with drawn batons, re-formed and charged again. The strikers dispersed.

Among the exhibits at the Grampian Police Black Museum is a container with locks of long blonde hair in it. The hair was from the head of eight-year-old Helen Priestly, victim of a child murder case that was later described as 'the finest example of scientific detection in Scottish police history up to that time'. The scientific evidence led to the conviction of Mrs Jeannie Donald for Helen's murder and to a sentence of death by hanging. This was later commuted to life imprisonment.

Little Helen and Jeannie Donald lived in the same tenement flat at 61 Urquhart Road, Aberdeen. On Friday 20 April 1934, Helen was sent on an errand to a nearby shop. She never returned. About five o'clock on Saturday

The Corn Market in Hadden Street at the turn of the century. When the Corn Exchange building became overcrowded, farmers spilled out on to the pavement and street and carried on their business there. The Corn Market was held in Hadden Street until the late 1950s, when traffic congestion forced it to move to the mart at Kittybrewster. Picture by courtesy of Aberdeen City Libraries.

morning her body was found in a sack in the lobby of the tenement. Her private parts had been interfered with, but later medical examination showed that there had been no sexual assault.

There were eight families in the tenement. The Donalds were the only people who showed complete lack of interest in the tragedy and failed to take part in the Friday night search for Helen. Both were arrested, but the husband, who had been working when Helen had died, was released. Jeannie Donald denied any knowledge of the crime, but when Sir Sydney Smith, a leading expert in forensic medicine, was called in, a formidable case began to build up against her.

The sack in which the child's body had been found was similar to others found in the Donalds' flat and fibres from the sack matched with others from the flat. Strands of Mrs Donald's hair were found in the sack and traces of Helen's blood were found in the accused's home. There was also a curious clue from an old practice of washing cinders, something often done by thrifty householders to make them last longer. Washed cinders were found in the sack, sticking to Helen's clothing, and in a box under Mrs Donald's sink. She was the only householder in the tenement who was in the habit of washing cinders. When the jury went out they took only eighteen minutes to return a verdict of 'Guilty'.

There were other horrifying child murders. In July 1963, the year in which Henry John Burnett was hanged, a seven-year-old boy was reported missing from his home in Justice Street. Four months passed before the remains of his body were found in the greenhouse of an allotment in Castlehill. This grim discovery also led to the solution of another child killing that had taken place more than two years before, when a six-year-old girl was murdered at Woodside.

The pieces of this jigsaw came together when another boy, also six, was questioned about indecent offences against him at the Castlehill allotment. He revealed that the lad from Justice Street, who had been his best friend, had also visited the allotment, drawn there by a man who had been in the habit of giving them money and sweets. The man was a 39-year-old labourer, James John Oliphant, who, when arrested, admitted causing the deaths of both children. He was also charged with assaulting a third child by trying to hang him with a rope and a hook, and with other offences against children. Because of his mental state the charges were reduced to culpable homicide and he was ordered to be detained for life in the State hospital at Carstairs.

There are some cases that have remained unsolved. The Betty Hadden Mystery is still a mystery — more than forty years after a forearm and hand were found on the south side of the navigation channel, opposite Greyhope Road, on Wednesday, 12 December 1945. They belonged to 17-year-old Elizabeth Hadden, daughter of a well-known Aberdeen prostitute, Kate Hadden.

Betty Hadden had been seen alive on the previous day, but there were indications that she was killed in Torry between midnight and five o'clock on Wednesday morning. Terror-stricken screams were heard in an area near the south bank of the River Dee at two o'clock in the morning. A sawn-off arm and hand were the only parts of Betty's body that were ever found.

The most sensational crime of this century had its roots in the Mearns, the rolling, gentle farmlands of Lewis Grassic Gibbon's *Sunset Song*. It was billed as the crime that shocked Scotland — the trial of the century. It certainly had all the ingredients needed to catch and hold front-page headlines during the summer of 1968 and the darkening days of November and early December. There were stories and rumours about illicit love affairs, kinky sex, high living, nudism — and murder. The key figures in the tragic triangle were Maxwell Garvie, a wealthy young Mearns farmer with a taste for flying and fast cars; his wife Sheila, an attractive brunette; and Brian Tevendale, a motor mechanic,

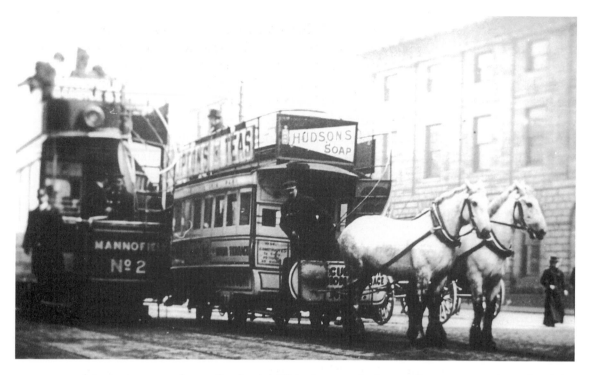

A transport era ends, another begins. This photograph shows a Rosemount tramcar drawn by a pair of greys alongside a Mannofield tram converted to electricity. Electric trams were introduced in Aberdeen in 1899, the Woodside route being the first in operation. By the middle of 1920 all routes were electrified.

Modesty boards were installed on the upper decks of open tramcars early this century. They were there so that ladies venturing on to the top deck could do so without fear of embarrassment. Note the advertisement for Hudson's Soap. Other popular posters advertised Fry's Cocoa, Beecham's Pills and Colman's Mustard. Picture by courtesy of Aberdeen City Libraries.

whose father had had a distinguished military career and had owned the Bush Hotel at St Cyrus.

Max and Sheila, married in 1955, had two daughters and a son, but during the early sixties their marriage began to break up. Max became interested in naturism, joined a North-east nudist group, and opened a club at Alford which was known locally as Kinky Cottage. Brian Tevendale became friendly with Garvie and introduced him to his sister, Trudy Birse, wife of an Aberdeen policeman. The four went out drinking together. Max went to Aberdeen to see Mrs Birse, Brian Tevendale was seen in the company of Sheila Garvie.

On 14 May, Max attended a meeting in Stonehaven. When it was over he drove off in his white Cortina. It was the last time he was seen alive. On 16 August, Sheila Garvie and Brian Tevendale were arrested. Next morning, Maxwell Garvie's body was discovered in an underground tunnel at Lauriston

Castle, near St Cyrus. Six weeks later, Tevendale and Sheila Garvie were charged with murdering Garvie by striking him on the head with the butt of a rifle or an iron bar and shooting him in the head. Alan Peters, a friend of Tevendale, was also charged with murder, but was later released. The trial was fixed for the High Court in Aberdeen on 19 November.

The ten-day Garvie Trial is still talked about in Aberdeen. Newspaper headlines screamed out the sordid story as the evidence unfolded — 'Wife weeps in murder court dock'...'Mrs Garvie's death night story'...'Max shot in struggle with wife on bed'...'Sheila Garvie tells of sex, nudism and pictures'...'The monster Max made me'...'Foursome became triangle'. Then came the banner headline that everyone was waiting for — 'Guilty'. On Monday 2 December, Sheila Garvie and Brian Tevendale were sent to prison for 'life'. Both are now free.

Public interest in the trial reached incredible heights. Newspapers printed page after page of evidence, yet it seemed as if they were feeding an insatiable appetite. The *Evening Express* sales rocketed to record totals. Long queues waited in the cold and wet to get into the court and those who didn't waited in Broad Street to get the latest editions of the paper.

When the trial ended hundreds of people gathered in Union Street in the hope of catching a glimpse of some of the main characters in the murder drama. Trudy Birse and her husband walked down the street from the courtroom to a national newspaper office and were mobbed. One vastly exaggerated report said there were 2000 people there. For a short time the routine lives of sober, respectable Aberdeen citizens were touched by unexpected excitement. Not everybody liked it; to many the crowds were vultures picking on the flesh of an unsavoury scandal.

Perhaps, looking back on it, there is a murky thread still linking us to the days when criminals were scourged, carted through the town wearing paper hats, and jeered or cheered as the trap-door of the scaffold opened up and plunged them to their doom.

CHAPTER EIGHT

My Lord Provost

Aberdeens's first Provost was Richard Cementarius, a mason, who held office in 1272. Since then, more than 160 Provosts have strutted across the civic stage, some making their mark on the city's history, others leaving little more than their names. Looking across the gulf of seven centuries, those early names seem strange to Aberdeen ears — Malcolm de Pelgoueni, who owned lands at Balgownie; Duncan de Malauill, or Melville; Laurence de Foty, who gave his name to Fittie; Alexander de Camera, or Chalmers; Andrew Scherar and Mathew Fichet. A more familiar name was Duncan Kynnedy. Kennedy was a common name in Aberdeen in the fourteenth century, as was Scroggs. If there are any Scroggs in Aberdeen today, they may be descended from John de Scroggs, the town's Provost in 1435. But they have a small skeleton in their cupboard. Provost Scroggs committed perjury during a hearing over the Earldom of Mar and was branded a 'hoary scoundrel'.

Five hundred years ago a number of prominent North-east families struggled for control of the city like a warring Mafia. Towering over them was the Menzies family. The first Menzies in the provost's chair was Gilbert, who was elected in 1423 and held office four times. From 1423 till 1634 the provost's chair was occupied twenty-eight times by members of the Menzies family. Four members of the family ruled over the city for eighty-three years. In 1590, an unsuccessful complaint was made to the Privy Council that free elections in the city were being perverted by the 'unlawful usurpation of the provostrie by the race of Menzies'.

The years are studded with the names of Provosts who made their imprint on the city's history — Robert Davidson, the hero of Harlaw; William de Camera, a member of the powerful Chalmers family, who got permission to build the first Town House on the site of the present Tolbooth tower; the Kintores, the Rutherfords and the opulent Cullens, a merchant family. Provost Andrew Cullen dealt in such things as 'Gyngar, pipper, cloys and blak bonetis', while his brother, Provost John, sold salmon and wool.

Later came the nineteenth century and Victorian Provosts, who created the modern Aberdeen — Thomas Blaikie, who laid the foundation stone of the New Market in 1840; George Thomson, Jr., who founded the Aberdeen Line and scrawled his signature across the great sailing ship era; Alexander Nicol, owner of Aberdeen's first clipper, the *Scottish Maid;* and Peter Esslemont, whose monument is Esslemont and Mackintosh's store in Union Street. There were many more.

The nepotism of the Menzies family had faint echoes in the first half of the nineteenth century when two brothers, Provost James Hadden and Provost Gavin Hadden, held office. James Hadden was known as the 'father of the city' because of his role in the building of Union Street and King Street, although much of the credit was due to his business partner, Thomas Leys of Glasgoforest, who chaired the meeting at which the decision was taken to open up the city west and north of the Castlegate. Leys held the civic chair from 1797–8 and 1803–4, while Hadden served as Provost for four terms, the first starting in 1809.

There were allegations that the Haddens 'kept their seats warm for family successors', for between 1798 and 1819 a number of their relatives and friends held Council posts of one kind or another. In 1819, a report on burgh reform said that Provost James Hadden had been fifteen times on the council; another business partner, Provost Alexander Brebner, had been ten times; and his brother Gavin ten times, while many members were 'chiefly either relations or connections in business with Provost Hadden'.

An Aberdeen bookseller, Provost Alexander Brown, also had long service on the Council. He was a Hadden supporter and was in the civic chair for two terms. An old rhyme ran:

> For twenty lang years in oor braif toun,
> Its affairs were maistly ruled by A. Broon;
> Or ane o' the Haddens wore the croon,
> And when Gavin gaed up, then Jamie cam' doon.

In the nineteenth-century line-up of Provosts, one man stood above them all — Alexander Anderson, regarded by many as the city's greatest civic head. He served a double term as Provost, and during his time in the civic chair was heavily involved in railway development in the North-east. The bitter war that raged between competing concerns was crowned by a plan nicknamed 'The Circumbendibus'. It was also called 'The Rubislaw Suburban', which must have sent a shiver of dismay down the spines of affluent West End dwellers, whose granite mansions were thought to be immune from such commercial invasion. The idea was that the Great North of Scotland Railway would be linked to the Aberdeen Railway by a line running from Woodside and Stocket Hill to Queen's Cross and Carden Place, then down the south side of Albyn Place to Guild Street, with a number of tunnels *en route*. The plan was thrown out.

It was Anderson who proposed, at a public meeting, the erection of Marochetti's statue of the Prince Consort, which now stands in Union Terrace. It was unveiled at the north-west end of Union Bridge by Queen Victoria in

October, 1863. It got a poor reception. People said that all you could see of Prince Albert was a huge pair of jackboots. The day began in pouring rain, but ended happily for Anderson. After she had pulled the cord on dear Albert's statue the Queen knighted the Provost.

The ceremony was significant for another reason — it was the first time that the title Lord Provost was used. At one time, the city's civic head was called Alderman, and later simply Provost. Alexander Anderson wanted to be addressed as 'The Right Honourable the Lord Provost', but there was no legal justification for the 'Right Honourable' tag.

Provosts were always addressed as 'My Lord', a convention that still exists, and magistrates were called 'Sir Bailie', 'Your Worship', 'Your Honour', and even 'Your Wisdom'. If that had been perpetuated it would have been ripe material for a 'Scotland the What?' script. The Provosts' lamps, another symbol of civic authority, first appeared in 1838. They raise curious contrasts. Two of these elegant lamps stand outside what was the home of Lord Provost James R. Rust in Hamilton Place, while another pair can be seen, only a few steps apart, at the entrance to a flat in Bonnymuir Place where Provost George Stephen once lived.

The traditional chain of office first draped a Provost's shoulders in 1760. Chains of office or not, bailies and provosts have not always been regarded as sanctified mortals living up to the title of 'Your Wisdom'. When Bailie Moggin, one of the characters in William Robbie's *The Heir of Glendornie,* was showing off his Provost's chain of office to a local merchant, he said it was a symbol of the power of the civil magistrate and should be 'a terror t' evil doers an' a' praise an' protection t' such as do weel'. The merchant remarked drily that there was a good deal of difference between what should be and what was.

The money for the first chain of office came from 'The Common Good', a fund which was established after the granting of the Stocket Forest to Aberdeen by Robert the Bruce. It has always been a source of controversy. In 1988, the Council clashed with the Secretary of State for Scotland over the use of Common Good cash for the new Leisure Centre at the Beach. As far back as 1491, when John Cullen was Provost, the Common Good was said to be 'in a most deplorable state', but today it is in sound financial standing. In 1817, there were complaints about the irresponsible 'hole-in-the-corner' manner in which the fund was managed by the Council; the public, it was said, were kept in complete ignorance of what happened to the money. They are no better informed today.

Despite the new municipal buildings in Broad Street and the lofty offices of St Nicholas House, Aberdeen folk still think of the Town House as the building topped by the steeple with the 'The Toon Hoose' clock. Between this tower and the Old Tolbooth are the city's sheriff courts and, above them, the Town Hall and its offices. The Mannie o' the Well stands across the street.

Cynical ratepayers nurture the thought that a lot of the Common Good cash goes on wining and dining. This probably springs from the fact that civic receptions are funded out of the Common Good. It is certainly not a new complaint. The historian John Spalding, who was Commissary Clerk of Aberdeen during the Covenanting troubles, wrote about magistrates wasting the Common Good in feasting and wine drinking. In 1866, a councillor called George Brown raised a motion against 'feasting and drinking at the cost of the public purse'. He also lashed out at the 'treating and banqueting' which went on under the Incorporated Trades banner. More than a century later, the sumptuous 'Trades' dinners are still going strong.

William Robbie had a word to say about Common Good feasting when Aberdeen celebrated the anniversary of the birth of George III in 1802. 'The magistrates of these days were loyal to the backbone, as we say, but on the principle, we suppose, that men are never more liberally disposed than when they can be generous at another man's expense, or dip their hands into the public purse, so, on no occasion was the loyalty of the Aberdeen Magistracy more prominent than when it took the form of consuming large quantities of liquors, and solids as well — the latter in the shape of "partan claws" and such like dainties — the cost of the whole being, as a matter of course, defrayed out of the Guild Wine Fund, a benefaction which the hospitality of a former age has provided for this special purpose.' (The Guild Wine Fund, originally held by the Burgesses of Guild, passed into the keeping of the Council.)

That Royal birthday celebration ended in a riot when a crowd of boys in the Castlegate threw mud at officers of a Ross and Cromarty regiment which was stationed at Castlehill Barracks. The officers, who had been drinking the King's health in the Town House, called out the troops. When a crowd gathered, shots were fired and four people were killed. According to Robbie's account of the affair, Provost James Hadden's action prevented an even worse catastrophe — 'he jist gaed richt in afore the baignets (bayonets) and teuk haud o' the muckle Heilan' sergean' 'at was leadin' them on, an' order's 'im t' call aff the sodgers direckly'. When the sergeant asked who he was, the Provost showed him his chain of office — 'the man kent at ance 'at *that* representit a pooer 'at daurna be triflet wi'.'

There was another Castlegate riot during Provost James Milne's term of office, but this time the Provost took action against the crowd. He led a charge of police into a mob of roughs who had shattered almost every pane of glass in the Town House. Yet Provost Milne, who was nicknamed 'Birdie', was never cast in the heroic mould. He was the 'excellent octogenarian Whig' who played host to the Circuit judge Lord Cockburn in his 'queer, out-of-the-way, capacious old-fashioned house' at No. 65 Gallowgate. He had a negro *major domo* called 'Black Tom', who ruled the roost in the Milne home. He and his wife were said by Lord Cockburn to be 'nice, kind, respectable, natural, happy bodies'.

Lord Cockburn told how during his visit Mrs Milne noticed that her husband's old brown wig, which was much the worse for wear, lay askew on his head. She leaned forward and adjusted it. 'Madam,' said the Provost solemnly, 'I'll thank you to let my wig alone, *I never* meddle with yours.'

Provost Milne, according to Lord Cockburn, had an accent and dialect of 'great purity'. What he really meant was that 'Birdie' spoke with a broad Aberdeen accent. The Aldermen of old were chosen because they were 'lele (loyal) and of gud fame', and they had certain conventions and courtesies to follow, but nobody ever told them how they should speak. During this century, civic heads have found the Doric an advantage rather than a drawback. Visitors to the city warm to a Provost who can greet them with a friendly 'Fit like? Foo are ye?'

Sir James Taggart and Sir Thomas Mitchell, who served as Provosts during the two world wars, were well-known for their use of the Doric. Tommy's broad Aberdeen tongue and his down-to-earth manner made him popular with the people. One newspaper, in fact, called him the People's Provost. Little Alex Collie, who could lapse into his native tongue with the best of them, was another civic chief who was popular because he fitted everyone's image of an 'ordinary' Aberdonian.

When the 'Postie' Provost, George Stephen, published a book of verse, *When the Nichts are Comin' Doon,* he asked Clement Attlee to write the foreword. The bemused Prime Minister must have struggled valiantly with Provost Stephen's description of 'lowsin time' and 'kitchie deems' and 'dowie nicht shades'. It was, as George himself said, 'a muckle moofu' o' braid Scots'. Attlee, choosing his words carefully, wrote: 'Some of his verses will be a little difficult for the English to understand.'

The Provost was not put out. He had no time for people who liked to 'pit it on', to speak in an affected manner:

> We may connach decent English en' wir
> mither-tongue as weel,
> Gin we pit it on to mak' folk think we're byously genteel.

connach — destroy; *byously* — exceedingly

Speak the Doric, he urged, and ignore criticism — 'We sanna care a docken (anything worthless) tho' the knabbery (lower class of gentry) gi'es a froon.'

Lord Provost Taggart was known as a superb storyteller. His greatest rival was Lord Aberdeen, who also had a reputation as a raconteur. On a number of occasions they appeared together on public platforms to compete against each other for the title of Prince of Storytellers. The old 'mean Aberdonian' myth figured largely in their repertoire. Typical of the quickfire Taggart quip was the story about the Aberdonian who went off on a month's holiday with a dark green shirt and a pound note and changed neither of them.

When he became Provost in 1914 (he served till 1919) he started a recruiting campaign and raised a brigade of artillery which came to be known as 'Taggart's Own'. He once told the story of how the King 'took the pledge' when war broke out. 'As Lord Provost of Aberdeen I did likewise. I never thought the war would last so long. Shortly after this the Boys' Brigade collected bottles for patriotic purpose and I allowed them to store them in my yard — seven or eight lorry loads of bottles. One day I overheard a carter who was passing remark: "I thocht oor Provost was a teetotaller".'

Before Lord Provost Taggart appeared on the civic scene, one of the first to make his mark on the new century was Sir Alexander Lyon, who became Lord Provost in 1905. He was in the chair when King Edward and Queen Alexandra visited Aberdeen in September, 1906, for the delayed quatercentenary celebrations of Aberdeen University. He played a leading role in the laying out of the Westburn and Stewart Parks and Union Terrace Gardens, in the development of the tramway system, and in the improvement of the Beach.

Lord Provost Lyon's career is set out in volumes of cards and newspaper cuttings which he meticulously kept over the years. Today, these scrapbooks are in the possession of his grand-daughter, Mrs Helen Keir, and they add up to a remarkable record of service. There are personal cards, including one from the Prince of Monaco; a card marking the opening of Aberdeen's 'new slaughter market' at Hutcheon Street; another with an invitation to 'a Conversazione in the Art Gallery' during a conference of Scottish bakers; and cuttings on the opening of the new Aberdeen Post Office and a garden party for 3000 people in the Duthie Park when the Fleet came to town.

There is also a cutting of the Address given by Lord Provost Lyon when he took over the civic chair. He told how he had been a member of the Council since 1885, and had sat under six Lord Provosts. He spoke of the widening of Union Terrace and his regret that so little had been done 'for the other side of the Denburn Valley'; of the tram service, with its 'cheap fares and clean cars' (all now gone); of the laying out of the city parks; and of the efficient police force and a fire brigade 'second to none'.

He thought they were at a period in their history when they should say 'Enough for the present'. They could drive the municipal coach too fast and bring it to grief. Yet he looked forward to improvements in the Gallowgate, the widening of Union Bridge and Broad Street, development at the harbour, and to fresh laurels being added 'to the already world-wide fame of the University'. I wonder what he would have thought about it all a century later.

Sir Alexander was a keen mountaineer and a member of the Cairngorm Club. Another hill-lover who was to follow him into the Provost's chair in 1932 was Sir Henry Alexander, author of the classic book, *The Cairngorms*. Provost Alexander edited the *Aberdeen Free Press*, his family's newspaper, until it amalgamated with the *Aberdeen Daily Journal* in 1922. It was during his time

The Prime Minister and the Provost, each in his own way a man of the people. Sir Winston Churchill, cigar in mouth, is seen with Sir Thomas Mitchell when he came to Aberdeen in 1946 to receive the Freedom of the City and be given the honorary degree of LL.D. by the University. Churchill, who had first visited Aberdeen in 1904, was given a rapturous reception by the public. Picture by courtesy of Aberdeen Journals.

in office that plans were drawn up for the laying out of Kincorth and the building of the ring road, Anderson Drive.

At one time, Provosts were forbidden to bake and sell bread inside their houses during their period in office. It was considered demeaning to their civic standing. Curiously, bakers were not held in high regard three or four centuries ago. Provost Alexander Jaffray's grandfather was a burgess of the baker craft and his lowly position rebounded on his grandson when he became Provost in 1636. It was said, with some contempt, that he was not one of the 'auld blood' of the town, but the 'oy (grandson) of ane baxter (baker)'. On the first Sunday after his election he went to church and found a baked pie on his seat.

If the same kind of civic snobbery had existed today, Provost Mitchell and Provost Collie might have found loaves of bread on their seats when they went to the kirkin' of the council. Both were bakers. Tommy Mitchell was a bit like 'Birdie' Milne; one newspaper writer who heard him speaking at a meeting of the Council commented, 'He chirps, positively chirps'. He was popular with the Press, which is not always the case these days.

Tommy, born in 1869, was the illegitimate son of an Oldmeldrum hotel owner's daughter and a police sergeant. He was fee'd on a farm before being apprenticed to a baker at a wage of thirty shillings for a half-year's work — and his 'keep'. When he started in business on his own in Aberdeen he was the youngest master baker in the city. He had two shops, one in George Street, the other in Queen Street.

He was a shrewd businessman, and in some ways was the prototype of the canny Aberdonian, 'kennin' the right side o' a shilling'. His attitude to money was probably shaped by his childhood, for as a boy he had a persistent fear of landing in the Poorhouse. One of his friends was a prominent businessman called Watt Hepburn, who was reputed to be a multimillionaire and knew how to get the best of a bargain.

One night, having wined and dined sumptuously in the old Trinity Hall, they were making their way downstairs when Watt Hephurn slipped and fell:

'Ooo-oh!' he groaned. 'I've twisted masel'!'
'Impossible!' cried Tommy.

It was said that when the two friends visited the Lake of Galilee on holiday, Tommy asked a boatman how much it would cost for a row on the lake. When he heard the price he remarked to Watt Hepburn, 'No wonder the Lord walked on it!'

Like Sir Thomas, Alex Collie disliked fuss and pretension. When he became Lord Provost, some people thought he was the wrong man for the job. He showed them that they were mistaken. His greatest asset was that he liked *people* — and they liked him. He was never dismayed by the great occasion. When he was representing the city at an oil conference in Houston, Texas, he turned up at a formal reception wearing sandals. I often saw him at a social occasion chatting away with a glass of whisky in his hand, totally unaware that most of the company had gone home to their beds.

The nineteenth century was a period of great change, much of it inspired by the city's Provosts, many of whom were knighted for their municipal work. The first half of the twentieth century produced another clutch of knighthoods, but Sir Thomas Mitchell was the last to be honoured in this way. Apart from Lord Provost John Smith's elevation to the peerage (he became Lord Kirkhill after helping to steer the city into the oil age in the 1970s) the post-war years have produced no Town House honours.

The Provosts of pre-war years, like those of the Victorian era, were business leaders as well as civic leaders. It is sometimes said that the Council today is run by trade union leaders — and people in retirement. Few of the city's top businessmen are prepared to give up their time to municipal work. The end of the war brought a swing to the Left in the Council Chamber.

The city's first Labour Lord Provost was Duncan Fraser, a sombre, unsmiling man, who ran a drapery shop in Schoolhill. He was elected in 1947, and since then control of the Council has virtually remained in the hands of the Socialists.

There have been some able men at the helm in recent years, but there is little doubt that the council of today lacks charisma. It certainly lacks 'characters'. There are no more Taggarts and Tommy Mitchells, no more Fraser Macs, 'G.R.'s' and Tom Scott Sutherlands. Councillor W. Fraser Macintosh was a fiery little Socialist, a familiar figure in a red bow tie and waistcoat, who in pre-war years was always being thrown out of the Council Chamber. It usually took an Inspector and four constables to eject him. In 1925, he sued the Lord Provost, Sir Andrew Lewis, the Council and the Chief Constable, for the sum of £20 as compensation for the 'suffering and indignity' he had endured when they evicted him. He withdrew the case in court.

'G.R.' was George R. McIntosh, whose figure made him the Ernie Bevin of Aberdeen; a broad, bulky man who punctuated his conversation with 'D'ye follow me?' Not everyone did, but G.R., a 'jiner' to trade, and proud of it, didn't mind. He often handed out little samples of his joinery work — tables and chairs — to charities and to his friends, among them the local Press. George was a frequent visitor to the news room of the two papers in Broad Street. He had a dry, quizzical wit which not everyone understood, least of all King George VI. When he was presented to the King at Aberdeen Joint Station, 'G.R.' said, 'We've got one thing in common. You've got the same initials as myself'.

On the other side of the political fence was T. Scott Sutherland, who, as some people said, was always leaping to his foot on a point of order. They didn't mean it unkindly, for Tommy Scott Sutherland himself made a play of the fact that he had only one leg. He lost the other one as a schoolboy. He could have used an artificial leg, and sometimes did, but he preferred to use his crutch — it was his trademark.

He dashed around like a latter-day Long John Silver, and some of his business ventures had a piratical touch about them. He was an architect by profession, but he tried everything from a cure for asthma to television, whisky and an 'infallible' cure for baldness. He himself had closely-cropped reddish hair which added to his unusual appearance. In his leisure-time, as if to prove that he was as good with one leg as other men were with two, he played tennis, swam and danced. His legacy to Aberdeen and to architecture was the Scott Sutherland School of Architecture at Garthdee.

W. WATSON   BALLATER

It would have made good material for a 'mean Aberdonian' story or a 'Scotland the What?' skit — a Lord Provost of Aberdeen travelling on a tricycle instead of a civic Rolls Royce. The Provost was Sir Alexander Lyon, seen with his wife on holiday in Ballater. The picture was taken by the Royal photographer William Watson. Sir Alexander, who became Lord Provost in 1905, sat under six Lord Provosts before becoming one himself.

One man who tried Tommy Scott Sutherland's baldness cure was the Battling Bailie. Frank Magee got the nickname from Winston Churchill when he stood unsuccessfully for Parliament. 'How's the Battling Bailie?' Churchill once asked. The tag stuck to him. An Englishman, he had a great love for his adopted city, serving it as a councillor for thirty-three years. He was always known as Baile Magee even after the title had slipped into disuse.

The Aberdeen tongue never bothered him when he sat as magistrate in the police court, where the accent of some of his 'customers' was as thick as pea soup, but he recalled the difficultly that arose on one occasion when a charge was read out to an old man in the dock — 'that the accused had urinated against a wall of 21 Queen Street'.

'Fit's that ye say' asked the accused.

The charge was repeated, but it was clear that the old man didn't understand the meaning of the word 'urinated'.

The clerk of the court leaned forward and said bluntly, 'You pished against the wall'.

Bailie Magee asked him if he had anything to say. 'I was bursting,' replied the old man, adding, 'And I'm bursting now!'

He was hastily taken out of the courtroom. Later, Bailie Magee learned that he had committed the same offence all over the police station floor.

Aberdeen's pet poet, Deacon Alexander Robb, wrote a poem called 'The Marvellous Councillor', which appeared in the *Aberdeen Observer* in July, 1835. His subject was Councillor D— (he was never named) and it was obvious that the Deacon thought him anything but marvellous. Not only was he pompous, he tripped over his grammar:

> Above all the rest a new comet is blazing,
> A genius as brilliant and bright as the sun,
> And science and learning astounded are gazing
> At the wondrous effusion of Councillor D—

If Deacon Robb had written that 300 years earlier he would probably have had his knuckles rapped. In 1503, Robert Walker, who lived in the Gallowgate, was banished from the burgh for slandering an Alderman, while thirty years later a John Singer was hauled up for slandering the bailies and officials. He had to appear 'sarklane' (wearing only his shirt), bareheaded and barefoot, and carrying a staff and a knife in one hand and a 4lb. wax candle in the other, to ask the bailies' forgiveness. The staff and knife were hung up in the Tolbooth in an iron chain as a reminder of his misdemeanour.

Nowadays, it is open season on Provosts and councillors, always, of course, with one eye on the lawyer waiting round the corner with a libel writ in his hand. It was no secret that Lord Provost, R.A.R. Robertson, had no great love for the Press. His predecessor, Harry Rae (or *Henry* Rae, as he preferred to be called after his elevation to the chair), seemed to take it in his stride.

The Adventures of Councillor Swick _____ Charo

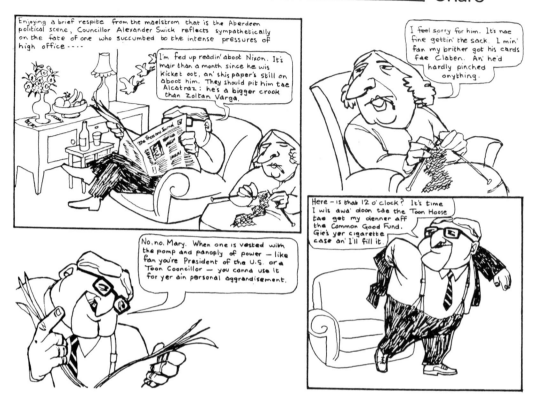

This is the face of Councillor Alexander Swick, who, having been introduced to an unsuspecting Aberdeen public on the stage, was given a visual identity by the 'Scotland the What?' team in a strip cartoon in Leopard magazine. Councillor Swick, who is apt to talk loftily about 'the pomp and panoply of power', has a sneaking likeness to someone we might know, but Buff Hardie and Steve Robertson are keeping tight-lipped about that.

I have always felt that Councillor Alexander Swick was in the Councillor D— mould. He loved to roll out phrases like 'the pomp and panoply of power' and to talk about the importance of education — 'we've all went to the school'. The councillor's home was in 'Scotland the What?' land; he periodically popped up in STW sketches, niggling us with the thought that he was suspiciously like someone we know. A 'swick' is a 'cheat', so you have to resist the temptation to make comparisons with living councillors, otherwise you might be hauled up in front of the bailies 'sarklane' and carrying a 4lb. candle.

The face actually takes shape in a strip cartoon, 'The Adventures of Councillor Swick', in *Leopard* magazine. Buff Hardie and Steve Robertson, who had already introduced Councillor Swick to the public on the stage, write the strip cartoon dialogue, while Aberdeen artist Sandy Cheyne does the drawings. There was a moment of panic when it was discovered that the cartoon character looked suspiciously like a real-life councillor. Some last-minute changes were made before they set him loose on the public. The Councillor was never too careful about what he himself said. 'There's one or two o' the lads on the Cooncil that disna ken naething aboot culture, the theeter or naething,' he once said. 'John Smith* himsel, thinks the Merchant of Venice is Luigi Stucchi's brither.'

Two well-known figures on the Aberdeen municipal scene, Robert Lennox, a former Labour Lord Provost, and Sandy Mutch, his one-time Tory rival on the Town Council, were the 'stars' of a Swick skit called 'The Bailie'. The charge was 'inscribing graffiti on a jetty at Fittie'. 'This graffiti is spreadin' a' wye,' says Councillor Swick. 'In St Nicholas Hoose, in the Lord Provost's private bog-cloakroom, the wa's covered wi't. Jist the other day I saw Robbie Lennox wi his aerosol can in his hand skitin' up on the wa' "Sandy Mutch is a big fat neep".'

The Granite City has come a long way since Aberdeen's first recorded Provost, Richard Cementarius — Richard the Mason — was following his trade by building a castle on Castlehill. It must have been hot, thirsty work. An early account shows that the sum of ten shillings was paid for carrying ten casks of wine from the harbour to Castlehill. Councillor Swick would have approved of that.

* Former Lord Provost, now Lord Kirkhill.

CHAPTER NINE

Poets and Printers

> Died here, in the second number of its age, 'The
> Aberdeen Citizen,' deeply lamented by the small
> circle of its friends.

This curious notice appeared in a notorious Aberdeen publication called
the *Shaver* on 9 January 1834. The *Shaver,* which had the kind of
reputation held today by the worst of the popular tabloids, was marking with
ill-disguised glee the collapse of one of its rivals. Nearly a century and a half
later, the *Citizen* was re-born. Its name was plucked from the past and given
to Aberdeen's first free newspaper, but its reincarnation was short-lived. In
1988, like its nineteenth-century namesake, it also vanished, only to re-emerge,
still a free sheet, as the *Aberdeen Herald.* Later still it became the *Aberdeen Herald
and Post.*

The span of 150 years has brought vast changes in the newspaper scene.
New technology has widened horizons for both publishers and readers, yet
there were far more newspapers and periodicals in Aberdeen early last century
than there are now. The public had a gluttonous, almost insatiable, appetite
for the written word.

'Aberdeen is the most newspaper-ridden community in the country,'
commented one nineteenth-century writer. Towards the end of the century
there were four dailies in Aberdeen, publishing ten editions, and on top of that
there were seven weeklies. The historian J. Malcolm Bulloch, himself a former
editor, carried out a survey of Aberdeen newspapers and periodicals in 1888
and found that the most prolific period was from 1830 to 1840, when no fewer
than twenty-nine newspapers and magazines were published. Twenty-two of
them appeared in the first half of the decade. The most productive year was
1832, when six appeared.

It was a period that produced a number of writers whose names still rank
high in the literature of the North-east. They learned their craft in the hard
school of journalism. Many edited newspapers, or contributed to the
apparently endless stream of papers and periodicals that descended on the
public. By the end of the nineteenth century, 160 newspapers had appeared
in Aberdeen. They came in all shapes and sizes, lacking nothing in
variety…news-sheets, 'quality' papers, scandal rags, academic publications,
political sheets — even so-called 'comic' papers.

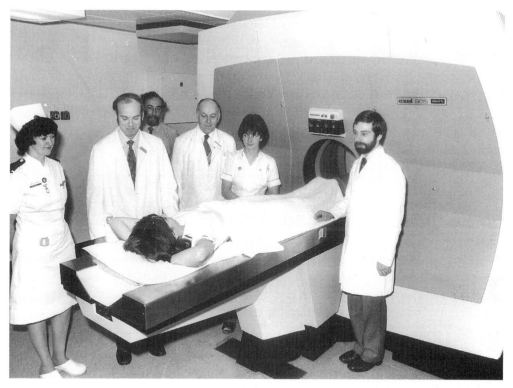

Laser Line, an appeal launched by the Evening Express, raised over £300,000 to buy this whole body scanner for the Aberdeen Royal Infirmary in 1981. The original aim of the appeal was to buy a gynaecological laser, but, when the money for this was raised in a matter of weeks the paper asked its readers to reach for a much trigger target — £28,OOO. The result of the appeal — one of many run by the newspaper over the years — buried for ever the mean Aberdonian myth. Picture by courtesy of Aberdeen Journals.

There was, as J.M. Bulloch pointed out, no great ingenuity shown in naming the papers. As some newspapers folded and others were launched, titles were often repeated. There were five *Aberdeen Magazines,* two *Caledonian Magazines,* two *Gleaners,* two *Examiners* and two *North Stars.*

Counting the modern free sheet, there were actually three *Citizens,* for the city Labour Party attempted to start up a *Citizen* between the two wars. It failed to make the grade. The Labour Party tried the same sort of thing a few years ago when they produced a municipal paper called the *Bon-Accord.* There had already been two *Bon-Accords,* the second a highly successful weekly paper. The civic *Bon-Accord* came in for heavy criticism and its publication was stopped, but it was re-launched.

Those early Press entrepreneurs thought up some startling names for their papers. For instance, there was the *Holloa!,* which lasted for only a few numbers before saying good-bye. The manager of *Holloa!* was C.A. Wilson, son of Aberdeen's pioneer photographer, George Washington Wilson. There were papers like the *Tyro* which were even less fortunate. Published in 1854, it made a solitary appearance and then vanished. Others in the oddity stakes were the *Water Kelpie,* the *Pedestrian,* and the *Bazaar Gazette, Unlimited.*

The area around Queen Street was the scene of most of the city's publishing activities. Byron, as a child, lived at No. 10 Queen Street before moving to 64 Broad Street. The street also housed one of Aberdeen's earliest theatres, run by an eccentric schoolmaster called 'Mad Sinclair'. The *Aberdeen Review,* published in 1843, was owned and edited by a Queen Street bookseller and newsagent, John Mitchell.

Nearby Lodge Walk, which has been largely obliterated to make way for Grampian police headquarters, was the home of a worthy called Alexander Ross, better known as Statio Ross or the Flying Stationer. He made a living by selling political and other pamphlets, which is how he came to be known as a 'stationer', but he won his own dubious place in local history by producing *Antiquities of Aberdeen,* which ran to thirteen parts — a penny each or 'the whole for one shilling'. When he insulted a local dignitary and was thrown into jail, he sent out this heartrending plea for assistance:

> My limbs are motionless, my blood is froze,
> The icicles are hanging to my nose;
> O Sirs, be quick, I'm standing at Death's door,
> Help, or your Flying Stationer's no more!

One paper actually gave its name to a street off Queen Street — Chronicle Street, later Chronicle Lane. The *Aberdeen Chronicle* was started in 1806 by John Booth, who won fleeting fame in a ballad about well-known local characters:

> He raised a sough wi' Johnny Booth,
> They'll baith get hell, an' a' that.

'Johnny Booth's paper', as it was called, lasted until 1832, when it 'quietly passed away' and was succeeded by the weekly *Aberdeen Herald,* which had its offices in Queen Street. The *Herald,* which ran for over forty years until its amalgamation with the *Weekly Free Press* in 1876, was one of the city's most influential newspapers, and the cradle of much of the literary talent that burgeoned in Aberdeen during the nineteenth century.

Under the editorship of James Adam, it became a powerful, campaigning newspaper. He was a portly, volatile figure. On one occasion he challenged one of his rivals, David Chalmers, editor of the *Aberdeen Journal* (and grandson of the founder), to a duel, but commonsense prevailed. The other side of his character was shown in his annual staff picnic, a happy affair which was duly recorded in the Poet's Corner in the *Herald* by William Cadenhead.

Cadenhead wasn't the only writer who cut his literary teeth on the *Aberdeen Herald*. The Inverurie poet William Thom had his 'Blind Boy's Pranks' accepted by Adam in 1841 and virtually shot to fame overnight. The Poet's Corner became the nursery of men like William Forsyth, who worked on the *Herald* as a sub-editor and later became editor of the *Aberdeen Journal;* David Grant, whose 'Muckle Spate of Twenty-Nine' has had a revival in recent years; William Carnie, also a sub-editor on the *Herald,* who wrote his three volumes of *Reporting Reminiscences* early this century; and a host of other minor poets.

Not all these nineteenth-century writers would find favour today. Much of Thom's work was cloying, full of 'dark and dowie glades', bursting bosoms and shining brows, while William Forsyth, who gave Aberdeen its Silver City tag, was at times unbearably sentimental — 'I'll love thee till my tongue be mute.' But their Doric poems endure...Grant's enchanting 'Muckle Spate'; Carnie's 'Hirpletillim', about an out-of-the-way spot in Rubislaw Den; and Forsyth's nostalgic 'Lover's Seat' — 'An' is't awa', that aul' stane seat that eased the Stocket brae.'

William Anderson's 'Jean Findlater's Loun', about a 'raggit loun' who 'dislikit the school an' cared mair for his play', was to find faint echoes seventy years later in Charles Murray's 'It Wasna his Wyte'. Anderson was a policeman poet, a one-time weaver who joined the police and rose to the rank of lieutenant. Like so many others, he was 'discovered' by James Adam. The Aberdeen of more than a century ago comes vividly alive in his poetry. He drew sharp, evocative pictures of the people and places he knew...Tibby Hogg, a dealer in cabbage; Gracie Finlay, 'wha dwelt i the brae' (St Catherine's Hill); Simon Grant, the town sergeant; and Archibald Black, a humpbacked wright:

> There are some yet alive min' on Archibald Black,
> The glazier an' vricht wi' a humph on his back.

In a poem to William Cadenhead he recalled how as a boy he had 'dooked' in the Raik, swum across the River Dee, taken a neep or a carrot from Innes's farm, and cut whistles 'free the boortree or ash' — the 'sappy sucker' that Hamewith wrote about in 'The Whistle'. He fished for fluke in the harbour and for seth (saithe, known locally as 'shittie sadies') and eel at Poynernook:

> We catched in the tide whiles the baddock and fluke
> Wi' the seth an' the eel at the auld Poynernook,
> Then their skins roun' our legs, as we ran owre the braes
> Wid aften prevent us free breakin' our tees.

(It was the custom for boys to wear the skin of an eel round their ankles to prevent injuries from stones.)

William Shelley was another policeman poet who was taken under Adam's

This gargoyle-like face once leered at passers-by from the wall of a tenement house at the corner of Broad Street and the now-vanished Ragg's Lane. It was put there by an eccentric shopkeeper called George Russell. Russell had it sculpted in the grotesque likeness of a neighbouring shopkeeper who had a disagreement with him. When the building was demolished in 1959 the gargoyle was moved to the south-east corner of Provost Skene's House. The city council seem to have deliberately hidden it away, for it is not easily seen and there is no explanatory plaque alongside it.

wing. It was said that he was 'swathed in poetry from head to heel'. Shelley, who had an unsettled, often unhappy life, was clerk in the Aberdeen Police Office. He sent his first contribution to the *Herald* in 1855, but it was not the kind of homely verse that Anderson produced. It mirrored something of the misery and poverty of his early years. One of his poems was called 'Poverty's Hame-come'. Shelley was a Londoner by birth, and lived for many years in England, yet it is his Doric poetry that stands out. For today's readers, his description of an old beggar man in 'Poverty's Hame-come' would resemble a

Doric test paper, full of phrases like 'tewed wi' wark' (fatigued), 'gloomed' (slept) and 'duddy gangrel' (raggit tramp):

> A fowsome coat hung frae him, 'tatter-wollops,'
> Happin' life's thrums, and creishie pocks forby
> His 'hither-my-dudds' o' breeks, a' clouts and scallops,
> Made corbies thankful for the power to fly;
> Through divers rents a kind o' sark was keekin',
> As gin it ettled mang the suds to be;
> Frae twa mismarrowed shoon his taes were seekin'
> And warslin' for a place to rest a wee,
> For, sooth, nae tender taes in siclike shoon could 'gree.★

★*fowsome* — fulsome, too large; *tatter-wollops* — fluttering rags; *thrum* — a tangle, mess; *creishie pocks* — greasy pockmarks; *hither-my-dudds* — ragged clothes; *mismarrowed* — mismatched; *warslin'* — striving.

While James Adam was encouraging his proteges at the *Herald* office, some less cultural activity was going on at Long Acre. This was where many of the city's printing presses were established. Not far away, on the site of the archway into Lodge Walk, Aberdeen's first printer, Edward Raban, set up in business in 1621. It was there that he produced the first *Aberdeen Almanac*, which was published up till about two decades ago and was the oldest periodical in Europe. There is a print museum in the Peacock Printmakers' premises off Castle Street.

But almanacs were never in the minds of the Long Acre printers early last century. In the year that the *Herald* made its appearance, a paper called the *Squib* was launched. It was Aberdeen's first 'comic' paper, and it headed a line of newspapers with strange-sounding titles and even stranger content. Most of them were published at Long Acre. Among them were the *Pirate*, the *Mirror*, the *Patriot*, the *Quizzing Glass*, the *Trumpeter* and the *Shaver*. This was the peephole Press of last century, forerunners of the so-called gutter Press of today. They traded in gossip and scandal, probed the private lives of well-known citizens, mocked the actions of a councillor called the Aberdeen Agitator, and carried scurrilous verses about old Bailie M—e.

From 1748, when the *Aberdeen Journal* was founded, to the late 1820s, most of the city's newspapers were conventionally dreary. The *Journal* talked pompously about holding fast to 'the principles of Church and State', and the *Aberdeen Chronicle* claimed it would always 'promulgate Truth — and that impartially'. Whatever their public stance, the solid citizens of Aberdeen, brought up on a heavy political diet in their newspapers, lapped up the snap-crackle-and-pop of this new kind of journalism.

Some papers sailed dangerously close to the wind, and were blown into the

A brick kirk in the Granite City! It sounds almost sacrilegious, but brick and granite rubble went into the making of Archibald Simpson's Triple Kirks, whose lofty spire rises above the Denburn. The three churches were the Free East, the Free West, and the Free South. Later, they became two kirks, latterly the East and Belmont Church and the Congregational Church of Albion and St Paul's, which were converted for commercial use. One became a restaurant named Simpsons after its architect.

libel courts. Others, unable to hold their own in the circulation war, went to the wall. Those that remained, particularly the *Shaver,* shed no tears. The *Shaver* reminded other possible rivals that the *Trumpeter* had started in 1832 with a weekly circulation of nearly 1000, but by August, 1834, had dropped to 400. In 1839, the *Shaver* carried the announcement: 'It is our painful duty to record that the first instance of mortality which took place in Aberdeen during the present year was that of the *Aberdeen Patriot,* at the tender age of two months.' The more respectable *Herald* wasn't exempt from this sort of backbiting. It had a formidable rival in the *Aberdeen Constitutional,* and when that paper fell by the wayside in 1844 the *Herald* reported it with black borders — and, it is said, 'with jubilant heart'.

They weren't all scandal sheets. The *Aberdeen Citizen* was one of the less virulent papers. It confined itself to demanding a public park for Aberdeen and criticising the way the bakers sold under-weight bread. It complained that the amount of bad meat sold in the city was due to the official concerned having too much work on his shoulders, and promised 'a revelation of the horrors of the Aberdeen "sweetie" trade'. The *Aberdeen Monthly Magazine*, which claimed to deal with important issues of the day, got itself involved in the Great Hat Case. This was a controversy over an allegation by Councillor Alexander Torrie that Bailie James Forbes had not only stolen his hat, but was actually wearing it.

The *Quizzing-Glass*, which was a fairly respectable paper despite its odd name, declared that it would publish anything 'calculated to amuse'. It was certainly not amused by the *Shaver*, and it published an attack on it by a writer who thought it contained nothing but 'disgusting ribaldry'. 'Falsehood, slander and obscenity meet the eye of the reader in every page,' he declared. 'It is a common sewer, collecting all the filth and slander of the town.' But, he added dolefully, many Aberdonians were delighted by it. Even worse, a lot of them were women.

At that time, Aberdeen's magistrates were having a purge on vice in the city, closing down brothels and sending their owners off to the Bridewell in Rose Street. The *Quizzing-Glass* bitterly attacked the attitude of the *Shaver*, which had described the attempt to wipe out brothels as 'a most unholy war'. 'Where are the inmates to go?' it asked. 'Brothels must be tolerated and encouraged as a substitute for a "house of refuge".'

The *Quizzing-Glass* also criticised the *Shaver* for an article it ran on the funeral of John Miller, the owner of a brothel in the Lochlands. The Press is said to have stirred up hatred against him. In 1826, he had to defend himself against a mob which surrounded his house, hurled stones at him, and chased him over a bridge on the Loch. When he died some six years later the same pious citizens crowded round his hearse, hooting, sneering and shouting — and all because he had operated a house of ill-repute. The *Shaver* said that on the Continent such a line of business was looked upon 'if not with approbation, at least without disgrace'. It thought that John had managed his house with 'much decorum and peace, considering the number of female boarders'.

The *Shaver* ran a column called 'Razor Cuts', which poured out malicious gossip about local people, mostly in high places. Often, instead of drawing blood from its thinly-disguised victims, it ended up with self-inflicted wounds. Case after case was brought against it for libel, and on one occasion it had to stump up £150, a considerable sum of money in those days, to Alexander Milne, a grain merchant. After that, it began to soft-pedal on its 'razor cuts', but its readership was on the slide, as well as its reputation. It claimed to have a circulation greater than 'all the three Aberdeen newspapers put together',

This picture by Aberdeen's pioneer photographer George Washington Wilson was called 'Cloud and Water Effects'. Wilson, with his photographer's eye, was obviously more interested in the play of light on the water than in the stricken vessel, yet behind the curious title lay a grim story. The vessel was a coal-laden schooner, the Queen, which was driven ashore on the beach at Aberdeen in March, 1883, during a fierce gale. The Queen was unable to make the crossing of the bar at the harbour entrance and a number of the crew, frozen stiff with cold, were blown off the rigging and drowned during the night. Picture by courtesy of Aberdeen City Libraries.

but eventually it faded away. The barber on the title page had cut himself once too often.

In 1837, the *Shaver* was back again — or, rather, the *Aberdeen New Shaver*. It lasted until 1840. It was badly printed and badly edited, and its content was even more venomous than that of its predecessor. The 'Razor Cuts' were still there:

> We would caution Miss M'c, daughter of an Upperkirkgate pawnbroker, to be more guarded in the company she keeps.

> When 'Daddy,' the coachman in Bon-Accord Lane, is out of a job, he ought not to employ his time in visiting and tampering with his neighbour's wife.

> An Advocate lad in Broad Street is advised not to pay so frequent visits to Mrs Craig, of Jopp's Court, as she no longer carries on business on the sly, but openly and above board.

We would hint to Archy the Architect that it is neither safe nor creditable to have his watch bandied about in Hadden's wool mill by a young woman whom he lodges with in an attic in Carmelite Street.

Married, at Wallace Nook, Joshua Hart, student in divinity, to Miss Ann Cumming, a very *obliging* lady.

Not all those early nineteenth-century newspapers were scandal sheets. The *Aberdeen Magazine,* founded in 1831, had contributors like John Hill Burton, who became Historiographer Royal for Scotland; the historian Dr Joseph Robertson; the Rev. J.B. Pratt, of Pratt's 'Buchan' fame; and John Ramsay, poet, friend of Wordsworth, and for a time editor of the *Aberdeen Journal.*

Ramsay, who was educated at the Grammar School, became a teacher at Gordon's Hospital (Gordon's College). One wonders what he thought when the *New Shaver* lifted the lid on 'certain doings in this princely establishment'. It alleged that during festivities at Gordon's one of the staff was 'seen to enter a water closet accompanied by one of his *female* guests, and they remained privately closeted for nearly half an hour'. Poor Gordon's, it was never out of the firing line. Ramsay occasionally wrote for the *Shaver's* arch-enemy' the *Quizzing-Glass,* but he also edited a slightly upmarket monthly called *Letter of Marque.* It carried 'Scraps' instead of 'Razor Cuts', and in one of them was a complaint that the Governors of Gordon's Hospital had employed a writing master to do part of the teachers' work.

The last decade of the nineteenth century saw the disappearance of the worst of the offbeat papers, although a few oddities still popped up. One was the *Meteor,* which flashed through the literary heavens and disappeared after one issue. It was intended to 'show light on dark subjects'. Two short-lived papers, published in 1886 and 1887, catered for the craze of the time — silhouettes. One was called *Silhouettes Galore,* which carried silhouettes of well-known citizens, the other was the *Monthly Cartoonist,* which had a 'Grand Jubilee Procession of Local Silhouettes'.

The *Bon-Accord* was published in 1881. It was supposed to provide 'a weekly budget of amusing reading'. Its appearance made J. Malcolm Bulloch think that history was repeating itself. For forty years Aberdeen had been without a weekly 'comic' paper; now the new *Bon-Accord* was signalling another change. 'The years 1830–40 produced nearly forty different periodicals,' he said. 'It would seem that the cycle had once more come round and that we are to be deluged with another shower of periodical sprouts.'

It was not to be. There were no more *Pirates* or *Patriots.* The *Bon-Accord,* said to be the first illustrated comic paper, lasted for eighty-five numbers, and a second *Bon-Accord* made its appearance in 1886. So one era ended and another began, stretching through the twentieth century to the computer age. In *Popular Literature in Victorian Scotland,* Dr William Donaldson said that what

A flashback to the glory days of the Aberdeen clipper. This photograph, taken in 1860, shows the outward flaring bows of the true clipper hull, first built in Aberdeen. The inventor was William Hall, seen fourth from the right. Picture by courtesy of Aberdeen City Libraries.

had virtually been a cottage industry in 1800 had developed by the end of the century into a large-scale capital-intensive business of considerable technical sophistication. No one could have visualised the technical strides that would be made in the following century.

Today, Aberdeen has two daily papers, the *Press and Journal* and the *Evening Express,* as well as a free newspaper which, after carrying the title of James Adam's paper — the *Aberdeen Herald* — became the *Aberdeen Herald and Post.* The 'P & J' is Scotland's oldest newspaper. It began as the *Aberdeen Journal,* a four-page weekly newssheet, under James Chalmers. It was turned into a morning paper in 1876, and in 1922 it amalgamated with the *Free Press,* becoming the *Aberdeen Press and Journal.* The *Evening Gazette,* owned by the Free Press group, disappeared, but the *Evening Express,* launched in 1789, continued.

The *Press and Journal* covers a vast area of northern Scotland and, with the coming of oil, has carved a powerful niche for itself as the businessman's paper. The *Evening Express* has an impressive penetration of Aberdeen homes, holding its own in a declining evening paper market. It has always had a close relationship with its readers. Just how close was shown in the Sixties and Seventies, when 'E.E.' readers raised thousands of pounds for a number of appeals launched by the paper. One was for kidney machines for Aberdeen Royal Infirmary, another for a body scanner. It also ran a highly successful 'Heart-Start' campaign to help heart-attack victims.

It is curious how the threads of past and present come together when you look back on Aberdeen's newspaper history. In May, 1946, the newly-appointed editor of the now-defunct *Weekly Journal,* which was part of the Aberdeen Journals' 'stable', was Cuthbert Graham, who was a sub-editor with the *Press and Journal.* Bert Graham had previously been assistant editor of the *Bon-Accord,* the paper which had been launched as 'The Illustrated News of the North'. When he took over the editorship of the *Weekly Journal* he started a feature called 'Mirror of the North' — and that was the title of a weekly paper launched in 1881.

In 1957 the *Weekly Journal* was closed down and Cuthbert became responsible for the morning paper's 'Weekend Journal'. It was here that he made his mark, not only in a weekly feature which took its theme from Sir Alexander Gray's 'Scotland' — 'This is my country, the land that begat me' — but in his bid to revitalise interest in North-east poets and poetry. James Adam's Poet's Corner was back, but this time it was called 'The North-east Muse'. It started in April, 1961. It began with the old names — Barbour, William Thom, Forsyth with his 'Silver City', Cadenhead and 'Kitty Brewster', Byron and his 'Lochnagar'. Charles Murray was given his rightful place. When his poem, 'There's Aye a' Something', first appeared in the *Press and Journal* in 1938, there was such a demand for it that several reprints of the newspaper had to be run off. There were names like John C. Milne, Nan Shepherd, Douglas Young and Helen Cruickshank.

But Cuthbert was also reaching out to a later generation of North-east poets, writers like Ken Morrice, who showed us Aberdeen coming to terms with oil in 'Boom Town' — 'Ile toon, boom city, Texas o' the North' — David Ogston, whose poem, 'The Share's Tale', was inspired by J.C. Milne's 'Fut Like Folk', Alastair Mackie, remembering his boyhood in the Thirties, and G.A. McIntyre, recalling the days of sail and how today's tall ships carry 'the same brave promise of prosperity from the wide sea'. The *North-east Muse Anthology* was published in 1977–78 and it was a delight to Bert Graham that one of its youngest contributors, Debbie Brewer, wrote the last piece in the book at the age of 12.

Dr Graham died in 1988. Some people felt that his work had not been sufficiently appreciated, or that recognition had come too late. Janet Murray, writing in the *Deeside Field,* said: 'There are few Bert Grahams about — let us not wait again until it is too late to eulogise.' So what was his contribution to

There is an old song that says, 'If ye're nae a Gordon yer nae use tae me'. Here, as they go marching through the city's main street, the crowds turn out to show that the folk of the Granite City certainly regard the cocky wee Gordons as 'the pride o' them a'.'

North-east literature? Flora Garry answered that question in a foreword to his anthology. 'He has brought poetry to the people,' she wrote, 'through our letterboxes and on to our breakfast tables. He has provided a rostrum for prentice and established poets alike. We are greatly in his debt; so is the community.'

The eighteenth century produced a string of writers whose talent was nourished by the smell of printer's ink, and this century has also had its quota. J. Leslie Mitchell, or Lewis Grassic Gibbon left school to become a junior reporter with the *Aberdeen Journal*. Later, Mitchell was to look back on his newspaper work in Aberdeen with nostalgia, remembering 'days that distance covers with a fine glamour'. It was in *the Journal* office that he was attracted to a girl called Margaret Miller, who worked in the front office. He wrote a poem to her:

And so I'll sing a song of Marguerite,
She who is lovely, smiling-eyed and sweet.

Unfortunately, Margaret had a boyfriend who was a sub-editor with a Liverpool paper. His name was George Fraser. They married, settled in Aberdeen, and George eventually became editor of the *Evening Express*. He was still writing a weekly column for the *Press and Journal* when he reached his century.

Another Fraser, G.S. Fraser, son of a well-known town clerk — learned his trade with the *Press and Journal,* first as a sub-editor, later as a reporter. 'I found that I had an eye and an ear, and could write easy, readable stuff, that was also accurate,' he wrote. His work as a newsman was reflected in his poem, 'A Letter to Anne Ridler':

But I was a reporter on a paper
And saw death ticked out in a telegram
On grey and shabby sheets with pallid print
So often, that it seemed an evening dram
Of solace for the murderer and the raper
Whose love has grown monstrous through stint.

Fraser went south to follow his career as a journalist and broadcaster, later becoming a lecturer in English Literature at Leicester University, but his thoughts often strayed to Aberdeen and the 'glitter of granite'. He was recognised as a poet of considerable note.

The Granite City has had its share of chroniclers. One of the early nineteenth-century historians was William Kennedy, an Aberdeen advocate, who produced *Annals of Aberdeen* in 1818. It had been criticised for its inaccuracies, but Kennedy faced an enormous task, for he had to examine masses of old deeds and documents, many of them in Latin. For some unknown reason, Kennedy was known as 'Stumpie'. He featured in a jingle about a brothel-keeper, 'Salmon Meg', who took shelter in St Nicholas kirkyard when chased by a mob — an incident that would have delighted the *Aberdeen Shaver* if it had been around at the time. What Kennedy had to do with it I don't know, but it went:

O. Stumpie, the lawyer, O. Stumpie, the laird!
They hae ta'en away Meggie, aside the kirkyard.

Other nineteenth-century writers who told the city's story included Walter Thom, James Rettie, Joseph Robertson and, perhaps the most readable of all from last century, William Robbie, who wanted to give Aberdonians 'a just and adequate conception of the history and progress of the city'.

The post-war years of this century gave us Fenton Wyness's *City by the Grey North Sea,* Cuthbert Graham's *Portrait of Aberdeen and Deeside,* and Alexander

Keith's A *Thousand Years of Aberdeen*. Keith's was the most exhaustive study of the city, a formidable work. 'A.K.' as he was known was leader writer and assistant editor of the *Aberdeen Daily Journal* after the First World War. One of the many editorial tasks he set himself was the editing of the ballad portion of the Gavin Greig folksong collection, *Last Leaves of the Traditional Ballads and Ballad Airs*.

He was a friend of Charles Murray and Dr David Rorie, author of 'The Lum Hat Wantin' the Croon', and he was a kenspeckle figure in the town. One of his last works was a book on *Eminent Aberdonians* for the Chamber of Commerce. He was probably too modest to realise that he himself had become one. When Aberdeen University conferred the honorary degree of LL.D. on him he was presented as 'the universal man of the North-east'.

With the new technology available in recent years, newspapers have been able to expand their operations and fight back against the competition of television. It is unlikely that Aberdeen will ever return to the 'newspaper-ridden' days of last century, but a new generation of writers will carve a different kind of niche for themselves in the century ahead.

CHAPTER TEN

Aberdeen at War

A fierce, red-bearded piper glowers down from the wall of a room in the Gordon Highlanders' regimental museum in Aberdeen's Viewfield Road The piper is the subject of a painting, 'The Gordon's Warning', by an Edinburgh man, G. Ogilvy Reid. For a time it was thought that it was painted by another Reid — Sir George Reid, President of the Royal Scottish Academy, who was one of Aberdeen's most distinguished artists. Sir George would have had an even greater claim to a place in the Gordons' museum, for the building housing the painting was once his home and studio. He bought it when it was known as Kepplestone Cottage, changing its name to St Luke's and bringing in the Aberdeen Architect Dr William Kelly to extend it.

St Luke's House dates back to 1800. Purchased by the Gordons in 1960, it was closed for a time for a new two-storey extension and was reopened in April, 1997. The gardens are laid out in the style of Lady Reid's original Victorian wall garden, with the type of flowers and plants she enjoyed. The information for these came from Sir George's paintings of his wife against garden backgrounds. In this modern, well-laid out museum, where huge windows are covered to protect fragile and faded battle Colours from the light that George Reid needed for his art, the arts of war dominate.

Sir George was only eighteen years old when he joined the City of Aberdeen Merchants' Rifles in 1859, and it was this company of part-time soldiers — the forerunners of the Home Guard — that inspired what was probably his first published work. It took the form of a pamphlet called 'Ye Nobell Cheese-Monger', an illustrated skit on the Volunteers, with doggerel verse poking fun at the old-style Dad's Army. Reid, who was an apprentice lithographer with a firm called Keith and Reid, drew the sketches of the Volunteers and their captain, William Stevenson, a local merchant, and may even have written the verses.

In a letter to an Aberdeen solicitor, Donald Sinclair, in 1907, he recalled nostalgically how in dark winter mornings he trudged for a couple of miles through snow and slush to attend squad drill by gaslight in the old Water House in Union Place. The Water House, which contained the reservoir for part of the town's water supply, was at No. 40 Union Place, which was eventually swallowed up by Union Street. The man in charge of No. 2 Company (1st Merchants') was a bearded Sergeant Munro, a retired soldier — 'one of the

The war was a month old when this picture was taken. It shows the 5th Battalion Gordon Highlanders leaving Bucksburn, on the outskirts of Aberdeen, on October 7, 1939, to board the train at Aberdeen Joint Station on October 7, 1939. 'To Heil with Hitler!' read the slogans on trains carrying the cocky wee Gordons to war. Picture by courtesy of Aberdeen Journals.

finest specimens of the old soldier I ever knew,' declared Sir George. 'Nothing escaped his eyes.'

By all accounts there was a definite Dad's Army air about the Merchants' Rifles. Reid recalled feeling distinctly uneasy when the muzzle of a rifle held by the man behind him played about the small of his back. 'The wonder is that serious accidents did not happen,' he said. 'The unsuspecting crowd of onlookers little knew to what dangers they exposed themselves.'

The Volunteers of 1859 were the forerunners of the *real* Dad's Army, the Home Guard. In the early days of the last war, like their military brothers of eighty years before, the Home Guard soldiers were also called Volunteers — Local Defence Volunteers. Until the change of name they were popularly known as the LDV, but the initials were open to other interpretations. A volunteer called Robert Pratt was having a drink in a pub with his mates when another drinker, taking a look at the group of volunteer soldiers, made a sneering remark about the LDV — the Low Down Volunteers. Private Pratt came smartly to attention and punched the offender in the mouth, breaking his jaw. He duly appeared at Aberdeen Sheriff Court, where the Sheriff summed up the case in half-a-dozen well chosen words — 'The man got what he deserved.'

There were Volunteers in Aberdeen long before young George Reid picked up his musket at the Water House. Whatever jibes they endured, there was never any doubt about their patriotism. In 1759, when there were fears of a French invasion (six French frigates with 1300 land forces on board appeared off the Aberdeen coast), an English publication called the *Gentleman's Magazine* carried a poem extolling the 'martial courage' seen in Aberdeen. It described how everyone from 'the honourable Mayor' to Johnny Barker, the scavenger, rallied to the call. They gathered '...like bees, in num'rous swarms, to learn the exercise of Arms'.

There were wrights, bakers, blacksmiths, barrel-troopers, masons and bricklayers; tailors dropping their needles and shears, fiddlers and pipers quitting their 'fiddle bag and grumbling drone', butchers putting aside the axe and knife, and carpenters laying down 'their squares and perpendiculars'. A force of 500 was raised on that occasion, and the *Gentleman's Magazine* declared:

> Tis hoped they'll make a bold resistance,
> And cause Monsieur to keep his distance,
> Should he attempt to land his host
> Upon the Aberdonian coast.

But Aberdeen had more than bagpipes and a grumbling drone to stir the blood of its citizens. Its own composers had their pens poised like spears. When the Aberdeen Volunteers were formed in 1797, John Ewen, a local jeweller, who wrote the well-known Scottish song 'The Boatie Rows', paid tribute to 'our brave Volunteers':

> At last we're completed, approved we have been,
> As a corps not unworthy of famed Aberdeen,
> And may we still hold it the pride of our years,
> To act with the spirit of brave Volunteers.

The call to arms in 1859 saw the *Aberdeen Herald* give space to patriotic purple patches from a contributor writing under the initial 'C'. This was William Carnie, who was a reporter with the *Herald* at that time, and the title of his poem was 'Nay! Never Say our Arms are Weak'. It struck straight at its readers'

Air-raid wardens and firemen search among the ruins of McBride's Bar in Loch Street, devastated in an air-raid in 1941. The bar was rebuilt and is still there today. In the same raid, Ogston & Tennant's soap factory — 'Soapy' Ogston's — was burned out. Picture by courtesy of Aberdeen Journals.

tear ducts, bombarding them with passages about the sleeping dead, swords hanging in their sheaths, hearts warm and true, and calling on people to gather 'from busy town and breezy down'.

Unbelievably, Carnie's piece of poetic extravagance was set to music and sung as a marching song by a corps of London Volunteers. There was no doubt that music was important to the Volunteers. One company, which boasted a brass and bugle band with 'chromatic attachments', rehearsed in the Spring Garden under an old military bandsman, Mr Campbell, while another band, led by Mr Reuben Hunter, a teacher of music, drilled in a hall in the Gallowgate, opposite Littlejohn Street, which for some unknown reason was known as the Dogs' and Monkeys' Hall.

Of course, not everyone was full of military fervour. Deacon Alexander Robb's book of *Poems and Songs* contained a number of anonymous verses all entitled 'Written on a Militia Schedule'. There is little doubt that it was Robb's own work. He may have used the militia schedule as a subterfuge to hide the fact that he was less than enthusiastic about military service. His attitude was probably summed up in the lines:

> To state objections, when I've none,
> Would prove myself a villain;
> I'm liable to serve, I own,
> But deevilishly unwillin'.

Men over forty-five were too old for military service, and another 'schedule' verse from Robb read:

> Militia laws, for mony a year,
> Hae vex'd me wondrous sair;
> But now, thank heaven, I'm clear, I'm clear,
> I'm forty-five an' mair

Like the more recent Home Guard, the men of the old-time Dad's Army never fired a shot in anger, but in 1805 a Lieutenant Booth, of the 1st Regiment of Aberdeen Volunteers, was killed at the Bay of Nigg in what was the last duel with pistols fought in Aberdeen. It happened when Booth's clerk, Robert Forsyth, a lad of sixteen, became involved in a brawl with an Ensign Livingstone, of the Stirlingshire Regiment of Militia. Livingstone drew his sword and stabbed at Forsyth, cutting his hand, and when Booth lodged a complaint about the attack the Stirlingshire man challenged him to a duel. The two men met at the Bay of Nigg at dawn on June 26 and Booth was badly wounded. He died after sixteen weeks of 'the most severe suffering'.

The Bay of Nigg was normally used as a firing range. It was there that the Volunteers tested their skills before the city organised regular Wapinschaws. The first was held in July, 1862. George Davidson, a local bookseller, wrote:

Aberdeen's wartime Lord Provost, Sir Thomas Mitchell, better known to everybody as Tommy, was flanked by two familiar faces when he celebrated VE Day in 1945 — Harry Gordon and Will Fyfe. The two comics are seen with the Provost (centre) at a Victory concert in the NAAFI in Market Street on VE Day. Picture by courtesy of Aberdeen Journals.

> And o'er the beach and waving bents,
> Far as the golden sands,
> The city's joyous thousands throng
> In merry laughing bands.

There was no poetic licence in Davidson's lines. It was estimated that at least forty thousand people turned up for the Wapinschaw, and 2500 soldiers from the Regulars, Militia and Rifles were on parade.

In 1865, the Sham Fight was introduced. The Enemy, totalling 1411 men, were supposed to have landed at the mouth of the Don and taken up positions in the middle of the Links. The Attacking Force, with 1560 men, were dug in at the base of the Broad Hill. This warlike situation was complicated by the fact that half the population of Aberdeen had taken up their own positions on top of the Broad Hill and on another height called the Cowhillock. Big guns boomed and rifles cracked and at the end of the day no-one was very sure who the victors were. Still, everyone enjoyed it…it was a sham 'Battle of Bon-Accord' that was to be repeated many years later under vastly different circumstances.

In 1884, Volunteer companies were linked to local territorial regiments and the Aberdeen infantrymen became the 1st Volunteer Battalion Gordon Highlanders. At that time, the 4th Battalion belonged to Donside. In 1914 the sham battles of the past became all too real. The *Evening Express* carried the headline DECLARATION OF WAR, and in the months that followed the paper faithfully recorded momentous events like the sinking of the *Lusitania,* when more than 1000 of the 2000 passengers died, alongside the minutiae of war. Eight young ladies, it was reported in May, 1915, had entered the Aberdeen Corporation tramway service as conductors.

In October, 1914, two Victoria crosses were won by Aberdeen men, both Gordon Highlanders. They were Lieut. Colonel J.A.O. Brooke, who was later killed, and Drummer (later Drum-Major) W. Kenny. From 1854, when Private Thomas Beach won the bravery award at Inkerman, the Gordons have chalked up sixteen Victoria Crosses.

In March 1915, 700 men of Taggart's Own, the City of Aberdeen Brigade of Artillery, raised by Lord Provost James Taggart, joined a parade of 4000 garrison troops in a parade through the city. Aberdeen's fishing fleet suffered badly during the First World War. In 1915, U-boats sank twenty-four trawlers in the space of two months. The city was blacked-out, as it was during the Second World War, but this was a precaution against sea attack, not air raids. The nearest Aberdeen came to an air raid was when a Zeppelin, the L20, lost its way, drifted inland towards Aviemore, then turned eastwards over Aberdeenshire and dropped bombs on Insch, Old Rayne and Craig Castle. The castle emerged unscathed. The Zeppelin passed over Newburgh on its way home, but apparently failed to spot the Granite City.

By 1917, Aberdonians were grimly chewing their way through an indigestible 'war bread', which had a creamy tint and was less dark than the standard bread of pre-war years. Meanwhile, in March of that year, Ramsay MacDonald turned up in town and was howled off the stage of the Music Hall by a mob of Socialist extremists. The audience refused to let him have his say; he spoke for eight minutes and then sat down. The chairman was told to 'Get into a kilt!' and the audience ended up throwing rotten eggs, onions and potatoes at the platform party. The most dangerous missile was a heavy seat thrown from the gallery.

It was a sight Aberdonians never thought they would see — a U-boat in their harbour. The date was August 7, 1945, the war was over, and sightseers flocked to Trinity Quay to see U776, a type V1 1c submarine which had hunted shipping off the coast. It had a 37mm antiaircraft gun on the lower gun platform and two twin 20mm cannon mounted on either side of the conning tower. Picture by courtesy of Aberdeen Journals.

The Volunteers came into their own again during the 1914–18 war. Volunteer training corps filled the gap when Regulars and 'Terriers' went overseas. The Aberdeen unit mustered over 1000 men. By 1917 the Aberdeen Volunteers had added an artillery section and a transport section to their strength. They were given a high-ranking seal of approval in 1917 when they were inspected by Lord French. Aberdeen had a flu epidemic in October, 1918, and doctors warned of 'depressing influences' after the illness. There were no depressing influences on November 11, when local newspaper headlines read — GERMANY ACCEPTS TERMS HOSTILITIES CEASE AT 11 O'CLOCK.

On September 3, 1939, the *Evening Express* produced a special edition the first time the paper had ever published on a Sunday. BRITAIN NOW AT WAR said the banner headlines, HITLER IGNORES LAST PEACE MOVES.

Along with major stories on the outbreak of the Second World War the newspaper carried a number of small 'fillers' — paragraphs dropped in to fill awkward holes in pages. They sat oddly beside huge black headings reporting the TOLL OF GERMAN BOMBERS (the latest report from Poland) and BRITAIN'S LAST WORD. Under stories about the blackout and Eire's neutrality a 'filler' reported a minor domestic crisis — Aberdeen Corporation transport department's receipts had shown a drop of £70 16s 8½d on the corresponding week of the previous year.

It was also reported that a Miss Marguerite Wilson had broken the Land's End to John o' Groats women's cycling record with a time of 3 days, 11 hours, 44 minutes. There was a brief item, headed 'Advice to Bathers', which, following a child's death in England, warned that an hour or an hour-and-a-half should elapse after a meal before a person bathed. Bigger blanks in the pages were filled by photographs of a peaceful rural scene at Midmar, a group of cyclists 'by the wayside', and two Buckie boys 'seeking adventure' on home-made rafts.

No-one looking at the Buckie picture could have imagined that 'adventures on rafts' would have a horrifyingly different meaning the following day. On Monday, September 4, it was reported that the liner *Athenia,* en route to New York, had been torpedoed off Ireland, with many Aberdeen people on board. Among them was nine-year-old Ruby Mitchell, an Aberdeen schoolgirl, who was making the crossing unaccompanied. Little Ruby, whose widowed mother lived in Toronto, had been on holiday to her grandmother, Mrs Kirton, 125 West North Street, Aberdeen, and her aunt, Mrs Skinner, 97 West North Street.

The Local Defence Volunteers, later to become the Home Guard, were formed in May, 1940. There were three Aberdeen battalions, the 4th City of Aberdeen Battalion, the 6th (Post Office) Battalion, and the 7th (Works) Battalion. Pikes were issued in the early days of the war, which seemed like a ludicrous back-somersault to the early nineteenth century, when the Royal Aberdeen Volunteers had in their ranks the Gilcomston Pikemen and the Aberdeen Pikemen.

There was another link with the past when, recalling the Sham Fights of the 1860s, another 'Battle of Bon-Accord' was staged in May, 1942. This time, however, the Volunteers, instead of facing each other, lined up against two battalions of the 52nd (Lowland) Division, who were given the task of 'destroying' the Home Guard's defences. The Army umpires failed to turn up, but the Home Guard's own umpires, who claimed to be unbiased, watched the ebb and flow of 'battle' and delivered their judgement — the attackers had been totally eliminated.

Even better known than the LDV in those hectic wartime days were the ARP, whose initials stood for Air Raid Precautions. The citizens of Aberdeen,

This attractive building in Aberdeen's Viewfield Road is the Gordon Highlanders Regimental Museum. Originally called Kepplestone Cottage, it was re-named St Luke's House when it was bought in 1800 by the painter Sir George Reid, who brought in Dr William Kelly to extend it.

wearing wardens' helmets and armed with fire buckets and stirrup pumps, sat through the night listening for the distinctive throb of enemy engines and the long, wavering wail of air-raid sirens. When it came they scuttled to their Anderson shelters or huddled under hall stairways. There were concrete boxes in tenement 'backies' big enough to take all the tenants, but some people preferred to stay where they were.

The city had its first air alert *before* war broke out. On 3 August 3 1939, an airship — the *Graf Zeppelin* — appeared off Aberdeen, looking for all the world like the ghost of the L20 from the First World War. It could be hazily seen from the Beach, a shadowy shape just above the horizon. From Dyce, the home of 612 Squadron, an aircraft went out and photographed it. The German Embassy in London, after denying its presence, said there had been a navigational error.

The real thing came in March 1940, when a lone German plane flew high over Aberdeen. It was a painless initiation, for no bombs were dropped, but Aberdeen was to get its share of air attacks in the years ahead. It was bombed more frequently, although not more heavily, than any other city in Scotland, withstanding thirty-four attacks. They were mostly what were known as tip-

and-run raids, but 178 people were killed. During July 1941, there were three air raid 'alerts' in one night.

The summer of 1940 was a bad period. A bungalow in Tullos was damaged by bombs on 26 June and Victoria Road School was destroyed when 100 incendiary bombs were dropped on Torry on July 1. Eleven days later, on 12 July, while people were leaving their shops and offices for their midday break, the city had one of its worst air raids. Lunchtime shoppers watched as a Heinkel bomber was chased over the city by three Spitfires. It jettisoned its bombs in an attempt to escape. The first stick landed in Aberdeen University's sports ground at King's College, another landed in a granite yard in Urquhart Road, and one blew a hole in the Beach Boulevard.

The last bomb landed on the Neptune Bar in York Place, crowded with workers having a lunchbreak from Hall Russell's shipyard. Thirty-four people were killed and seventy-four injured. The bomber, smoke pouring from its engines, went into a dive, narrowly missing Broomhill School and crashing into Aberdeen's new Ice Rink on South Anderson Drive. The ice rink was never completed. Houses now stand where the original rink was planned.

The bombers kept coming. Early in 1941 a name known to generations of Aberdonians became the target. 'Soapy' Ogston's — Ogston & Tennant's soap factory in the Gallowgate — was bombed and burned out. Another casualty in the area was the Loch Street public house called McBride's Bar. In April, 1942, bombs fell on the engineering works of J.M. Henderson and in August extensive damage was done in South Market Street and Poynernook Road.

Aberdeen hit the headlines in April 1943 — in a Berlin magazine 'So griffen wir Aberdeen an!' read the headline in the *Berliner Illustrierte Zeitung*, which carried a series of artist's impressions of a raid on the city on 21 April. Targets alleged to have been hit by the bombers were marked by arrows on an aerial photograph. One picture depicted a gunner firing at a 'flak' tower.

The two main sketches showed a squadron of bombers flying low over the centre of the city in close formation. In one of them twelve aircraft could be counted. Tracer bullets spun out from the bombers' rear and front gun turrets and great clouds of smoke blackened the sky over the city. There was the outline of a ship, presumably lying in the harbour. In the top sketch the bombers were shown at the start of a bombing run over Union Street. A building in the foreground looked like the Music Hall.

The attack on Aberdeen on Wednesday 21 April was the biggest raid of the war. The *Illustrierte Zeitung* made it look like a London blitz, and to Aberdonians it *was* a mini-blitz. Twenty-five Dornier 217s of the Kampf-Geschwader Group 2, stationed at Soesterberg near Utrecht in Holland, flew to Stavanger, refuelled, and took on their two-ton bomb loads. Dusk was falling as the Dorniers, coming in from the north, swept over the city and dropped their bombs.

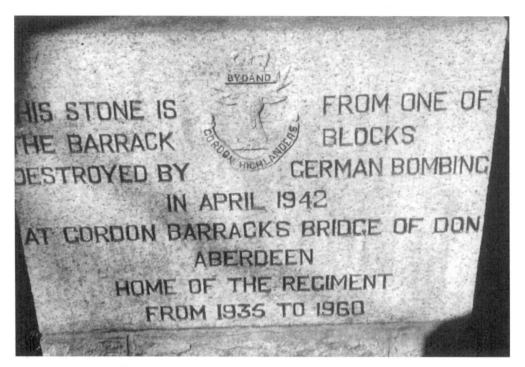

A granite stone near the entrance to the Gordon Highlanders Museum recalls one of the worst air-raids on Aberdeen during the last war. It is a stone from one of the blocks at the Gordon Barracks, Bridge of Don, destroyed by German bombers in April, 1942. As the inscription points out, the Barracks were the regiment's home from 1935 to 1960.

The raid lasted from 10.26 pm to 11.21 pm and the George Street part of the town took the brunt of the attack. The Elmbank and Froghall areas were hardest hit. Eighty-three-year-old Mrs Helen Farquharson, who lived in a top-storey tenement flat at 16 Elmbank Road, was in the back-garden air-raid shelter with her neighbours when a bomb fell four doors away. They had just got into the shelter when the bomb exploded. 'The whole shelter rocked,' she said. 'When we came out we didn't know what had happened.' As the dust and smoke cleared they discovered that a complete block of tenement flats had disappeared. There were six homes in the tenement; everyone in them was killed. The shock waves lifted the roof off No. 16 and the tenants had to be housed in other accommodation.

Cattofield suffered badly. Causewayend Church was severely damaged. Later, the pupils and staff of Sunnybank Primary School put up a memorial to five youngsters killed in the raid. The oldest was ten, the youngest five. St Mary's Episcopal church, the 'tartan kirkie', was badly damaged and bombs fell in the Westburn Park, near the Royal Mental Hospital.

The bombers also struck the Gordon Barracks. Twenty-seven soldiers died and twenty-six were injured. At the entrance to the Gordons' Museum in

Viewfield Road there is a memorial to these men — a granite stone from one of the blocks hit in the air-raid. The number of casualties at the barracks was never disclosed, but the official casualty list for the city was ninety-seven killed and 235 wounded. People still remember a funeral cortege winding its way down Seaforth Road to Trinity Cemetery at the burial of unidentified victims. Lord Provost Tommy Mitchell stood at the gravesides.

That grim night in April 1942 virtually marked the end of the aerial war as far as Aberdeen was concerned. The last 'raid' on the city was on another April day — in 1944. The intruding aircraft was sent scurrying for home when 'ack ack' guns opened up on it. The following month, newspapers carried the headline, GERMANY SURRENDERS. On 15 August 1945, the *Evening Express* reported that 'seething, singing, cheering, dancing, jubilant crowds' had packed the centre of Aberdeen after a dramatic midnight announcement that Japan had surrendered.

The streets rang with the sound of accordions, trumpets, saxophones and bagpipes — any kind of instrument that people could lay their hands on. Bonfires ringed the city, rockets shot parachute flares into the air, and the sky was lit up by searchlights that were no longer probing for Heinkels and Dorniers. Ships' sirens sounded out from the harbour, people rushed into the streets to shake hands, and fireworks crackled and flashed at the Gordon Barracks.

It was all over, not only the bombs and bullets, but the way of life that had become all too familiar during the war...the gas masks, the sirens, the firewatchers on duty in darkened shops and factories, the British Restaurants where you could get a meal for under a shilling, the blacked-out trains and blacked-out buildings. The lights were coming on again — and nobody would tell you to gobble up carrots because they improved your eyesight. Did anyone ever *believe* that? You could eat bananas instead — they were banned because ships were needed for more important cargoes. There would be no more sweet rationing, no more clothes coupons, no more shortages. It didn't all happen at once, but the thought and the promise were enough to be going on with.

CHAPTER ELEVEN
Ghosts in the Aulton

Aberdeen people have come to regard Old Aberdeen as an ageing suburb of the Granite City. There is little to show that it was ever a burgh on its own, run by its own Council, free of interference from its 'big sister' on the other side of the Spital Brae. Long before it was swallowed up by New Aberdeen, the folk of Aulton had a niggling fear that it might disappear as a separate community. They had always been fiercely independent, conscious of the fact that they had been given 'all rights, liberties and privileges belonging to a Citie'. In 1489, when James IV granted 'Ald Aberdon' a charter making it a free burgh of barony, it meant that they could appoint 'Burgesses, Provost, Baillies, Serjants and other Officers'. They did just that.

Until its amalgamation with the city in 1891, the old town had its own Provost and Council, its own coat-of-arms, its own Town House — still there today — and its own Cathedral and College. It even had its own Loch, just like the one in Aberdeen, although in the end it was a shortage of water from the Aulton loch that helped to bring about its downfall as an independent community. James Gordon, the mapmaking parson of Rothiemay, was a little dismissive about Old Aberdeen's status. Since it was a burgh of barony and not a Royal burgh, he said, that meant that even a pedlar couldn't set up shop there without a licence from New Aberdeen. It was more of a market town than a city. This sort of carping infuriated the Aulton folk. It was a proud town — and it didn't take kindly to interference from its uppity neighbours over the hill.

There was continual friction between the two communities. In October, 1672, Old Aberdeen sent a letter to the Privy Council complaining that Aberdeen magistrates were contravening Acts of Parliament dealing with the Old Town's 'liberties of merchandising'. The business of trading was often the cause of dispute. In 1772, in a court dispute between the Incorporated Trades of the two towns, Old Aberdeen alleged that the tradesmen of Aberdeen were always trying to overturn their freedom. They said that Aberdeen acted 'as if we were their suburbs'.

When the two towns amalgamated, Old Aberdeen took the decision through necessity, not from any fondness for the so-called *New* Aberdeen. The Town Council was short of funds for vital projects in the burgh. One of the major problems was that the water supply was inadequate. The springs supplying the

Facies Ciuitatis ABERDONIÆ Veteris. The Prospect of Old ABERDIEN.
This Plate is Most humbly Inscribed to The Rt Honble Simon Lord Lovat &c — Governour of Invernesse

This was Old Aberdeen, as engraved by Dutchman John Slezer in the 17th century, when it was a burgh in its own right. The familiar twin spires of St Machar Cathedral are silhouetted against the skyline, but also there is a third tower — the great central tower, built by Bishop Elphinstone, which collapsed and crashed to the ground in 1688. Another lofty landmark is the 'new' Imperial Crown of King's College. The original Crown fell to the ground in 1631, but a short time later it was 'built in a more stately form'. The Cromwell Tower, a fortresslike tower-house seen behind the eastern end of the Chapel (to the right of' the Crown), had twenty-four bedrooms. Near it is one of the two round defensive towers which stood there in the mid-17th century. One of the most interesting features of the lithograph is the Snow Kirk, at the bottom right of the picture. The Snow Kirk (*St Mary ad Nives*) was founded in 1497. All that remains of it today is part of its kirkyard, hemmed in by modern University buildings, with a handful of tombstones whose inscriptions are mostly in Gaelic.

burgh stood on ground that had been bought by the Great North of Scotland Railway, and the rest came from a burn running from the Loch of Old Aberdeen into the Powis burn, then crossing College Bounds and going down to the Links by University Road.

There was also the problem of street lighting. People wanted the street lamps lit every night in winter, but the cost-conscious Council lit them only when there was no moon. If the moon was shining- no lamps. As for maintaining law and order, the burgh's finances showed that they could afford only half a policeman -they shared a 'bobby' with the county! Better roads, better lighting and a better water supply would come only through amalgamation.

When Old Aberdeen was a free burgh of barony it had its own coat-of-ams, which can still be seen above the door of the Town House. The present Georgian building was erected in 1788, but the date on the panel is 1721, indicating that it belonged to an earlier town house on the same site. The Old Aberdeen coat-of-arms featured the Aulton Lily, which grew profusely in the area at one time.

The Council held a plebiscite, but then, as now, too many people were apathetic about local affairs. Nevertheless, there was a majority vote against union, but in time the two towns agreed to amalgamate. The necessary Act of Parliament was signed in 1891. King James's charter had made the Aulton a free burgh of barony 'for ever', but its independence was wiped out by the stroke of a pen. In 1603, the Council had ordered all residents to big (build) up their back-dykes 'for the outhalding of strangeris'. Nearly three centuries later, neither dykes nor decrees could hold out the strangers coming over the Spital from New Aberdeen.

James Gordon estimated that Old Aberdeen was one English mile or one Italian mile from New Aberdeen. Just to play safe, he threw in the additional information that the distance between the crosses of the two towns was 'a large Scottish mile', which must have had something to do with the canny Scot's habit of underestimating distance. Since then, countless generations of students have travelled over that 'Scottish mile' from Marischal College to King's College in Old Aberdeen.

It was at one time the main route to the north, but as you climb up the Gallowgate today, past the new Bon-Accord Centre and the towering monotony of Porthill Court there is little to remind you of its rich and colourful history. Fenton Wyness described the demolition of the Gallowgate as a major disaster, and the historical vandalism that has taken place there was given a final painful twist when the monstrous Mounthooly roundabout was built.

One road goes by Causewayend and Great Northern Road to Inverurie and the north, while another route branches off to the Spital and the Aulton. In the clutter of buildings and grassland to the right of King's Crescent is the site of what Gordon described as 'the sick house'. This was the Lepers' Hospital, standing on ground known as the Lepers' Croft. From here the lepers went into the city to beg for alms, swinging handbells to warn people of their approach and crying 'Unclean! Unclean!' St Peter's Hospital, founded in 1168 as a home for old priests and poor people, was on the site of St Peter's Cemetery.

From the top of the Spital Brae the road drops down through College Bounds to the High Street, running on to St Machar Drive, which it joins by splitting into two legs on either side of the Town House. This curious double-pronged approach to the main road is a leftover from the days before St Machar Drive existed, when one leg continued by the Chanonry and Tillydrone, following the River Don to Woodside, where it joined the road to the Garioch. The other leg turned east by Don Street to Balgownie, where travellers going north crossed the river by a ford. Later, the Brig o' Balgownie was built.

Gordon's map shows the Mercat Cross outside the Town House, marking the point where the High Street divides. The original cross was broken up in 1797, but towards the end of last century the top part of it was rediscovered. It was restored in 1950. It sat uneasily in front of the former St Mary's Church, which houses the university Geography Department, but it was eventually moved to a position in front of the old Town House.

There have been endless debates and discussions on what to do with the Town House. One room of it was utilised as a branch of the Aberdeen City Libraries. It could scarcely be described as an imaginative use of the building. The present Georgian-style structure was designed in 1788 and incorporates part of an earlier eighteenth-century building.

Its solid granite ashlar walls and its clock tower and cupola attract visitors to the Old Town. Over the entrance doorway is the burgh coat of arms, its Latin motto reading *Concordia res parvae crescunt* — By harmony small things increase — but a tiny barred jail window on the east gable suggests that harmony didn't always exist in the Aulton. There are few pieces of the Town House jigsaw to be found inside the building if you try to form a picture of what happened there three or four centuries ago. The top floor was used as a

The Town House at Old Aberdeen — a Georgian building erected in 1788. Three storeys high, it has a clock tower topped by a cupola. Over the entrance is the old burgh's coat-of-arms, dated 1721.

masonic lodge. In the library on the first floor there were a number of seventeenth-century chairs carved with the emblems of the five Incorporated Trades of Old Aberdeen, but these have now been removed.

A great deal of the history of the Aulton has its origins here, whispering tantalisingly through the rooms that occupy three storeys of the building, and it would have made sense to use the Town House both as a library and as a museum. The library's bookshelves carried only one volume of the two-volume *Records of Old Aberdeen,* a work that includes extracts from Council minutes going back to the start of the seventeenth century. In that tidy, book-packed room the voices of the bailies come rumbling out of the past. It was here in the Council chamber that the leaders of the Aulton community decided the fate of the townspeople, ruling on such weighty matters as markets and morality, crime and punishment, kirkgoing and Sabbath-breaking. Here, they decreed after the Reformation that no-one should go to the Snow Kirkyard to pray at their husband's grave because it was 'playne superstition'. The Church of St Mary ad Nives (St Mary of the Snows) stood where the Snow Church-yard is in College Bounds.) They imposed fines on people whose horses were found on their neighbours' grass and corn, and they indicted Isobel Jamieson for stealing 'ane sark and ane playid' from William Lindsay and Christian Craighead.

The shirt and plaid cost Isobel dear. She was ordered to be tied to the Mercat Cross and 'tirrit (stripped) fra the vest up', then scourged through the town and banished from it — 'never to be found within the Bishopric of Aberdeen under pain of death'. The whipping was carried out by an official scourger, who was paid eight shillings a week for his task. Old Aberdeen had its share of shady ladies. Another was Janet Cairnie, who was ordered to appear before the authorities to explain the 'odious and scandalous' conversations she had had with the town's scholars. Janet, being a sensible woman, fled from the Aulton before the wrath of the bailies descended on her.

Christian Grant was less fortunate. In 1720 she was banished for 'habitually recepting and haunting scandalous persones guilty of a great deall of prophaneness and wickedness'. Christian was one of the real-life characters plucked from the *Records of Old Aberdeen* by the writer Agnes Short and thrust into the pages of *The Heritors,* a novel which faithfully depicts life in the Aulton in the late seventeenth and early eighteenth centuries.

One of the leading figures in *The Heritors* is William Montgomery, who was banished from Old Aberdeen for molesting John Sledders and his family. Fiction rubs shoulders with fact in the novel when the enmity between Montgomery and 'the Sledder woman' explodes into vitriolic confrontation. The mason accuses Mrs Sledder of being a 'slanderous, evil-tongued witch', claiming that she has put the evil eye on his crippled daughter.

The official records show that Montgomery was twice banished for the same offence. He ignored his first expulsion and returned to Old Aberdeen to threaten Sledders and his family with 'mischieff'. He was put behind bars in the Tolbooth, but was freed after signing another voluntary act of banishment and agreeing not to molest or trouble the Sledders. The punishment for returning a second time was that he would be burned on the cheek and whipped out of the town by the hangman. Burning on the cheek or shoulder was a common punishment in the Old Town.

In *The Heritors,* Montgomery features prominently in the attempt to prevent the collapse of the St Machar Cathedral tower. St Machar had a prominent tower as well as its familiar twin spires at one time, but in 1688 the tower fell, shattering the transepts and eastern end of the Cathedral. It was said to be caused by Cromwell's men removing stones from the Cathedral to build Aberdeen's castle — 'The Englishmen taking away the walls of the chancel, which guarded it upon the East, to build the fortifications of the castle-hill at Aberdeen, anno 1652, or thereby'.

The man who wrote that was William Orem, town clerk of Old Aberdeen about 1725, who was the author of a history of the burgh. The collapse of the steeple, he said, 'broke the college and merchants' lofts, and many desks and gravestones in the church and the two isles, which had been laid upon persons of distinction, and covered with plates of brass, that were taken away when the church was robbed'.

It also 'raised coffins, made of congealed sand as hard as stone, wherein persons of note had been laid'. William Gall, the church beadle, tried to profit from the disaster by sifting the ashes of the dead during the night for rings and pieces of gold. Gall is described as a bellman in the *Records of Old Aberdeen,* where it is recorded that he was ordered to appear before the congregation and 'make acknowledgement of his fault' for his 'barbarous and inhumane act'. Orem observed that 'the said beadle never prospered one day after for so unchristian an act'.

The fascination of the Aulton is that its old wynds and closes look as if they had remained unchanged since Montgomery and the Sledder woman hurled insults at each other across the High Street. Some names, like Douglas Wynd, are still there; others have gone. Barely noticeable across the road from the Town House is Market Lane, a link with the market day and the old-time fairs. The Aulton Fair, or St Luke's Fair, lasted for eight days. It had caravans, coconut shies, fat women, calves with two heads and calves with no heads.

William Orem mentions some of the old streets, filling in interesting background details as he goes along. There was, for instance, Reid's Wynd 'at the end of the town as people pass to the Bridge of Don'. It was a 'broad green way to the links for the use of the clergy who lived in the Chanonry and Chaplain's chambers', but ordinary mortals were barred from it. In March, 1658 the bailies laid down that 'neither man, woman, horse, or foot, should pass down that road called Reid's road'.

Douglas Wynd gets a mention, along with Beverly's Wynd, Wagril's Wynd, Bartlet's Wynd and College Wynd. Orem also gives us a glimpse of building developments in the early years of the eighteenth century. Bailie Troup's house on the west side of the town had a platform roof which didn't keep out the rain, so he built a new roof above the 'platform' and covered it with tiles. Alexander Molyson, a local merchant, bought the north-east tower of the Chaplain's chambers and half of the green beside the Bishop's dovecot. He planted twenty-nine trees near the Chaplain's chambers and some young trees in the dovecot green.

The bronze and marble monument to William Elphinstone, Bishop of Aberdeen, who founded King's College in 1498, stands outside the Chapel, near the Aulton's High Street. In the background can be seen the tall, minaret-like towers at the entrance to Powis House. They were built by John Leslie of Powis about 1834.

The names of the inhabitants of 'Auld Aberdeine' in 1636 can be found in the *Records of Old Aberdeen*, so it is possible to make up your own historical identikit and attempt to fit faces to places. There were a number of wobsters (weavers) and there were two baxters (bakers), Alexander Wadie and Alexander Ortoun, while Elspet Jaffrey, Christian Hay and Margaret Boyes were breid-sellers. Isobel Kelman and Elspet Gray traded in food of a different kind. Isobel was a kailseller and Elspet was a puddinwricht, making oatmeal puddings. The list includes such curious names as laxfisher (salmon fisherman), shanker (stocking knitter) and commer (midwife).

Working wives were well to the forefront. Among them were a number of browsters (brewers). The Aulton Brewery was famous for its beer and ale. Queen Victoria, who liked her drop of whisky while staying at Balmoral, may even have tasted the Aulton brew. Katherine Trail, whose father, Professor

William Milligan, was the first to occupy the Chair of Biblical Criticism at King's College, recalled in *Reminiscences of Old Aberdeen* how the brewery sent its carts all over the countryside, including Balmoral.

'It was a great sight when a cart laden with barrels of beer, drawn by two splendid, beautiful groomed horses, their harness polished to the last degree of shine, set out with beer for Queen Victoria's household,' she wrote. 'The driver walked proudly at their head. It was a two days' journey to Balmoral and two days home again.' There is a sign at New King's indicating the site of 'The Old Brewery'. It is a permanent reminder of an Aulton worthy's remark when the building came down — 'We would hae been better wantin' the University than wantin' the brewery!'

The Aulton may have been quaint, but after dark it could also be fearful. Warlocks and witches stalked the streets, and ghosts and boodies chased each other round the lurching stones of the old kirkyard. There was more to the sough of the wind in the High Street than a mere change in the weather. In 1631 a 'furious tempest' blew down the Crown of King's College — and a man was accused of raising the wind that did it. A woman was also said to have 'come over the watter of Don without ane boat'.

Even in the more enlightened years of last century people were still glancing fearfully over their shoulders, and the reluctance of the Council to light its streets didn't help matters. There was one feeble gas lamp in the Chanonry and the nearest to that was at the Town House. The branches of tall trees cast long shadows over the gas-lit streets, and late-night travellers kept a nervous eye open for Spring-Heel Jack, who was said to roam the Chanonry and Chaplainry dressed in a white sheet. The only defence the lieges had against such terror was a timid policeman known as 'Sudden Death'.

There are more than ghosts in white nightshirts to haunt you as you walk the street of the Old Town today. Here, you are always made aware of the people who brought 500 years of learning to the Aulton...the founder bishop, William Elphinstone, whose bronze and marble monument stands outside the chapel; the Principals and Professors, the first Mediciner, the red-gowned students. Bishop Elphinstone's monument is a reconstructed tomb originally planned for inside the chapel. It carries a Gaelic inscription referring to 'our holy teacher, the man Elphinstone, scholar of the Gaels'.

The first Principal was Hector Boece, from Dundee, who was a Lecturer in Philosophy in Paris, and arrived in Old Aberdeen in the spring of 1500. He wrote of the new College that it was

> A statlie structure there,
> A fabric firm and fair.

The first Mediciner was James Cumming, who was instructed by Bishop Elphinstone to lecture his students 'in his own manse in Old Aberdeen, properly dressed, after the manner of the Parisian doctors'. As for the Professors, J.M. Bulloch said that a century ago 'our Profs were a homegrown lot, with homely ways and a Doric phrase', and many had their roots in 'crofts and country knowe'.

Behind the Profs and their students hovered the Sacrists, many of them ruling the roost at King's, showing scant respect for red gowns or black gowns. Katherine Trail recalled one sacrist called Speedman — 'Speedie' — a little, white-haired man who wore 'a most voluminous purple gown', and bearded, bowler-hatted James Colvin, who was a bit of a disciplinarian. Colvin was Sacrist at King's from 1872 to 1891 and at Marischal before that. 'He never became the mere servant,' said J.M. Bulloch. 'Danky' — Charles Dankester — a Cornishman, took over from Colvin.

This century also brought its quota of characters, men like John Harvey, who was assistant Sacrist from 1907 to 1 934. He is remembered for his meeting with Queen Mary when she arrived for her Honorary Graduation. She turned up a few minutes early and panic set in in high places, but Harvey calmly took out his watch, held it in front of the Queen, and said, 'Ye're ower seen, Yer Majesty'.

The red gowns of the students have gone from the Aulton, which seems a pity. The historian John Hill Burton mentioned them in a magazine article written back in 1829. It drew an interesting picture of the Aulton of early last century- 'the quiet, straggling streets...the old ivy-covered houses, sticking their gavel (gable) ends into the pathway, with the little pigeon-hole windows prettily painted green, crow steps at the end, and moss-covered flag-stones on the roof'.

Burton wrote of 'sturdy, weather-beaten old men, with broad bonnets, knee-breeches, and huge, red velveteen waistcoats reaching almost to their knees; old women with high-stopped mulches, sitting on huge stones at their doors, knitting the stocking...grave students wandering about in their red gowns and the professors stalking to their classes in their black'. That there is still a flavour of Burton's Aulton 160 years later is largely due to the restoration and preservation work carried out by the University, but the sight of Aulton folk at their front doors is something that belongs to the past, not the present.

John R. Allan, who was brought up in the Aulton, went to King's, and had a great love for the Old Town, was in two minds about the restoration work that had been done there. In some ways it was good for the town, but he was concerned not only that the University had bought up so many houses for their teaching staff, but that the intention was to transfer Marischal College departments to Old Aberdeen. His fear was that there would be nobody left but professors and lecturers and a few shopkeepers. 'I can't help thinking it would be a loss when the professor no longer lived next door to the scavenger,' he said, 'when there was nothing left in the Aulton but accents veneered over by Oxford and Cambridge.'

A gateway to both old and new . . . to New King's and the Old Brewery in Old Aberdeen.
This striking gateway on the High Street near King's College Chapel leads to New King's,
which, as the date shows, was designed in 1912. Beyond it is the modern building known as
The Old Brewery. The Aulton brewery, which stood on the site, had a fine reputation; beer
from the Aulton went to Balmoral Castle. The name is also perpetuated in nearby Brewery
Lane.

Trees cast their shadows over the Chanonry as students walk to their studies at King's College. In the days of gas lamps, there were stories about ghosts haunting the Chanonry. Lined at one time with manses, and now with professors' houses, it was directly linked to the High Street, but now St Machar's Drive cuts through the old road.

The University's severe financial problems brought a halt to the policy of buying up every piece of property that came on the market. Nevertheless, it seems as if John Allan's worst fears have been realised, and that the Aulton *has* become a University precinct. The mixture that John Hill Burton saw, where Aulton folk sat at their doors and watched the academics go by, certainly has no modern counterpart. The 'scaffie' has moved on. Instead, the University has had a mushroom spread in Old Aberdeen sprouting departments in every direction…halls, lecture theatres, student accommodation, botany and forestry departments, buildings for everything from recreation to computing science.

No matter what changes take place in the future, it is unlikely that the Aulton will ever lose its magic. It is hard to put a finger on its special quality. John Hill Burton said it was 'quite remote from the new town', and perhaps it still is, even if Aberdeen does now act as if 'we were their suburbs'. Katherine Trail was once asked about the atmosphere of Old Aberdeen. She said that when you came down the Spital Brae and saw the Town House and the twin towers of St Machar you felt as if you had been transported into a different century, almost a different life.

Hector Boece, coming from Paris to this grey northern town, probably wondered if he had done the right thing, and even 'our holy teacher, the man Elphinstone', must have had doubts about establishing a university for 'men who are rude, ignorant of letters and almost barbarous'. Yet in the end both men were captivated by the Old Town. George Rowntree Harvey, literary and drama critic of the *Press and Journal* before the last war, once peeled away the centuries and attempted to listen in on a conversation between the Bishop and Boece. This is what the Bishop said:

> I love this place, all seasons of the year.
> Men of the south who do not know its charm
> Think of our northern Aberdeen as only
> A tent of skies that has its differing shades
> Of grey; as a haunt of snow and rain, of winds
> Aye snell — little they know who do not live
> Upon our seven hills and taste the sweets
> Of every season here! No other place
> I've known sees autumn come with richer gold,
> With lovelier tapestries at dawn and dusk.
> Often it seems to me our autumn here
> Is but the birth of spring, thoughts of decay
> Can never flourish in this seaward place.

The lines are from *Good Maister William Elphinstone,* a chronicle play written by Harvey and broadcast from Aberdeen in June, 1931, as part of the celebration of the quincentenary of the birth of Bishop Elphinstone.

Across St Machar Drive from the Town House is the Chanonry, running down by the Cruickshank Botanic Gardens to St Machar Cathedral and meeting up with Tillydrone Road. Up this 'cassied' road, the old route to the north, is Benholm's Lodging, better known to Aberdonians as the Wallace Tower. In 1963 it was taken down from its site in the Netherkirkgate and rebuilt stone by stone on Tillydrone Hill.

Whatever attention visitors pay to the Wallace Tower, few give much thought to the grassy mound at the summit of the hill. Yet if you scramble up its slopes you will be on top of the Motte of Tillydrone, the site of a twelfth-century timber fort commanding a ford of the River Don. William Elphinstone probably stood on that lumpy little hill 500 years ago, looking out over the lands of Seaton. He would have had a different view of the Don, for Parson Gordon's map of 'the Old towne of Aberdone' shows the river sweeping farther to the east, curving through what is now the centre of Seaton Park.

Winter puts a snowy cap on the familiar twin spires of St Machar and the gravestones in the old kirkyard. The picture was taken in 1871. There are tombs in St Machar's Cathedral dating as far back as the 16th century. The original church was founded by St Machar (Mochreibh) about AD 580. The churchyard is enclosed by 18th-century walls and the gate lodges were designed by John Smith in 1832. Picture by courtesy of Aberdeen City Libraries.

There is a fanciful tale that the knoll on Tillydrone Hill was built up by nuns, who, as a penance for some sin, carried up soil from the low ground of Seaton in their aprons. There is also an old legend about the founding of St Machar's Cathedral…that St Machar was told by St Columba to establish a church on the River Don where its meanderings took the form of a bishop's staff — 'besyd a watyr bank that ran into the sea', as the chronicler John Barbour put it, 'lyk a byschopis staf had been'.

The story has been discounted, for the river has so many twists and turns that the Cathedral might have been built anywhere. But, looking at both river and church from the Motte of Tillydrone, it is tempting to believe that St Machar saw something that inspired him to choose this spot on the banks of the Don to establish the Cathedral whose twin spires have been a symbol to generations of Aulton folk, as well as to their neighbours in New Aberdeen.

CHAPTER TWELVE
Century of Progress

A distant rumble of war marked the start of the century that gave us two world wars and the atom bomb. While thousands of people turned up in Aberdeen's Castlegate to usher in the twentieth century, their celebrations were muted by thoughts of what was happening in South Africa, where names like Ladysmith and Mafeking were finding their way into the history books. A sombre reminder of the times could be found in Esslemont & Macintosh's store in Union Street, where they were selling Priestley's Mourning Fabrics in their Mourning Department. Still, life went on, and there were other problems. One shop was doing brisk business with an ointment called Mother's Help — a 'sure cure' for nits.

In those war-anxious years, 'Victoria,' the great bell in St Nicholas Tower, rang for about five minutes to greet the new century, but its booming chimes were to become a requiem, not only for the war dead, but for the Queen whose name it carried. Victoria's grandson, Prince Christian Victor, who was serving in South Africa, died of enteric fever in October 1900, and in November the Queen attended a memorial service for him in Crathie Church. 'My tears flowed again and again,' she said. The old Queen was failing. She drove round the cottages at Balmoral for the last time. 'I have come to say good-bye to you,' she told her servants.

Queen Victoria died on 22 January 1901. There were half-drawn blinds in shops throughout Aberdeen, the city churches were draped in black, and the Town Council called a special meeting to pass a resolution on the death of the Queen. The Victorian era had come to an end; now a new and challenging age lay ahead. No one could have foreseen what sort of impact it would have on the Granite City, but before the twentieth century was over Aberdeen was to be dragged out of its insularity and thrust into the unaccustomed role of an international oil town, the Houston of the Northeast, a place where the broad accents of the Aberdonian mixed with the Babylonian tongues of Americans, Dutch, French and Norwegians. It was estimated that at one point there were 40,000 of them in this North-east corner.

During the twentieth century the city was to claim international status in other areas: in music, for instance, with its international youth music festival, and on the international soccer field. The first international match ever played in Aberdeen took place between Scotland and Wales at Pittodrie in February,

A solitary No. 44 tramcar on its way to the Bridge of Don, a horse and cart at the kerbside, a man crossing Union Street pushing a wheelbarrow…it's not the sort of scene you would see in Aberdeen's city centre today. This was Holburn Junction, 1908. No traffic lights, no cars no traffic wardens. The west end of Aberdeen's main thoroughfare was known as Union Place until the end of last century, when it was swallowed up by Union Street. The 'Billiards' sign on the right of the picture marks 'The Divan', one of the city's most popular billiard saloons in the first decade of the present century. Picture by courtesy of Aberdeen City Libraries.

1900. It was said to be 'the finest football ground out of Glasgow or Edinburgh'. Some 12,000 people turned up for the game — and Scotland won 5–2.

Ten years later, the Dons took part in a game that still has echoes in today's encounters with the Old Firm. In September, 1910, they met and triumphed over Rangers at Ibrox — the first time they had ever beaten the Blues. The *Evening Express* greeted the victory with the sort of exuberance that had marked the relief of Mafeking. 'Year after year the Aberdeen men have striven to carry a brace of points away from Ibrox,' it reported. 'The fall of Rangers is another proof of the decline of the two great Glasgow combinations, the long-continued domination of the Celtic and Rangers having apparently received a check.' Ninety years later, the Dons are still challenging the dominance of 'the two great Glasgow combinations'.

The towering statue of Major-General Charles Gordon - Gordon of Khartoum — stands guard over the archway at the entrance to Robert Gordon's College in Schoolhill. There is another Gordon statue at the end of the long avenue behind the archway —-the marble statue by John Cheere of Robert Gordon, placed in a niche above the entrance doorway to the 'Auld Hoose', the original college building.

In 1983, Aberdeen reached for the stars — and came home from Gothenburg with the European Cup-Winners' Cup. It was a bit like VE Day all over again, for this victory in Europe made stolid Aberdeen citizens go wild. Thousands turned out to welcome them home; there were 20,000 people at Pittodrie to see them arrive with the trophy. They should have strewn the streets of the Granite City with roses that day, for Aberdeen also gathered an international reputation as the City of Roses. It won so many Britain in Bloom contests under its leisure and recreation director, David Welch, that it became embarrassing (it was debarred for a time from taking part in the contest). David, who gave up the post in 1989 to go to a post in London, should have been given a bouquet of roses before he moved on, but he would probably have tipped his hat to his gardening forbears, who paved the way at the turn of the century.

The Westburn Park was opened in 1901 and the Duthie Park in 1883. The Duthie Park was beginning to bloom with Spring flowers in April, 1913, when horrified keepers discovered that there had been some unofficial cutting outside the Wintergardens, or what was known then as the palmhouse. The words 'Release Mrs Pankhurst' had been carved out of the grass in 12ft. by 3ft. letters. The Suffragists, who were at the height of their campaign, had also painted large black letters on the palmhouse door reading 'Votes for Women'. There was even a 'terrorist' attack in Aberdeen. A suspicious-looking canister was found at the Joint Station, with a lighted candle inside it. If it had burned down it would have ignited some inflammable material and set off a charge of gunpowder.

The turf-cutting at the Duthie Park paled into insignificance alongside what happened on the turf at Epsom Downs two months later, but there was an Aberdeen connection. A well-known Suffragette called Emily Wilding Davison rushed out of the crowd and threw herself in the front of Anmer, the horse carrying the King's colours in the Derby. The woman, who had the Suffragette colours tied round her waist, was knocked down, and the horse turned a somersault, falling on its rider. The jockey escaped serious injury, but Emily died a few days later. It later emerged that she had already been arrested for acts of militancy. She was sentenced to ten days' imprisonment at Aberdeen Police Court for assaulting an Aberdeen clergyman with a dog whip at the railway station. She thought he was Lloyd George.

Aberdeen had a typhoid epidemic in 1912. It was nothing like the one that hit the city half a century later, but there were twenty cases and it caused a good deal of anxiety. In 1919 the authorities were faced with another medical crisis, and this time it led to the Great Haircuts Riot. The school medical authorities had power to take and clean any children infested with vermin, and on this occasion they had been wielding the scissors on the heads of girls at the Middle School. Irate mothers complained that the cutting had been done

The 'Auld Hoose', the original building of Robert Gordon's College, with John Cheere's statue of the founder above the entrance. This was where Robert Gordon founded his Hospital for poor boys in 1720, although it was 1750 before it actually became a boarding school. Before that, in 1746, it was occupied by the Duke of Cumberland's troops. They called it Fort Cumberland.

without any warning and on June 16 over 2000 of them gathered outside the school in protest. Stones were thrown and windows broken. Next day, schoolboys and girls demonstrated at the Middle and other schools and a number of women gathered outside the gates of the Middle and demanded admission.

The police were called in and by eight o'clock in the evening the Gallowgate was blocked by a mass of men and women. Attempts were made to rush the entrance, but the police, ducking a barrage of missiles, held them off. Police reinforcements were called in and at eleven o'clock at night a last attempt was made to rush the entrance. It failed, and the crowds went home. Two days later the 'strikers' were back at school. The 'Tak' a's' (attendance officers) chased up the missing youngsters. The older boys were given the 'scud' (strap), with the severest belting going to those who had to be rounded up from their homes.

The statue of Byron was undamaged when fire raged through his old school a few years ago. Byron was a pupil at the Grammar School from 1795 to 1798. The Grammar, which originally stood in Schoolhill, was built in Carden Place in 1863. Its architect was James Matthews and the builders were said to be mostly elderly men, some of them in 'tall hats and swallow tail coats'. Despite doubts about the desirability of restoring the fire-damaged school, it was decided that the Grammar would be restored to its former glory.

The year 1926 saw the opening of a new Woolworth's in Union Street, with its 'Nothing over Sixpence' sign prominent above the door. The sixpenny offer also applied inside the store's cafe, where for a humble 'tanner' you could get a choice of fresh salmon, fricassee of veal, roast pork, or Yorkshire pudding. If you were hard up you could settle for a plate of soup for threepence — or a sweet for the same price. There were 20,000 articles on sale at sixpence or less. Today, 'Woolies' is still going strong, but it would be surprising if you found *anything* there at sixpence — and a miracle if you found anything at less than that.

Not many stores remained in Union Street as long as 'Woolies', which is now in the Bon-Accord Centre. 'E&M's' is still there, although its Mourning Department has either vanished in a flutter of black crepe or has been reincarnated in more subtle disguise. But stores that were as distinctively Aberdeen as the Town House and Edward VII's statue — that 'fat clort wi' the doos' shite on his brou', the Aberdeen poet Alastair Mackie called it — are no longer with us, although one of them, Falconers, shelters under the umbrella of the House of Fraser, which could be in Sauchiehall Street or Princes Street or any other Street of Multiples. Watt and Grant's has gone, along with Isaac Benzies in George Street and the Rubber Shop in St Nicholas Street. I never yet found out why it was called the *Rubber* Shop.

The changes have come in different ways, sometimes with the subtlety of a clenched fist, crunching through the guard of anyone who stands in the way of progress; at other times more furtively, like a thief in the night, so that you wake up one morning and find that your heritage has gone. I leaned over the parapet of the bridge at Rosemount Viaduct and wondered what happened to Schoolhill Station, where the 'subbies' stopped. It was the last suburban station before the 'Joint', and there was an oft-quoted and slightly *risque* Aberdeen joke about making sure that you got off at Schoolhill. Down below the bridge, behind HM Theatre, is an ugly parking lot leading to Union Terrace Gardens.

At the west end of Schoolhill, they have been torn down the Triple Kirks, Archibald Simpson's masterpiece in brick, which Lord Cockburn called 'a rude Cathedral-looking mass containing three Free Churches'. These were the East, West and South Free Churches. The east preaching hall became a restaurant in 1974, taking its name — Simpsons — from its architect. The spire, which is a copy of one of the twin spires of St Elizabeth in Marburg, Germany, still reached gracefully to the sky, defying suggestions that it was unsafe and should be brought down, but early in 1998 there were moves to develop the site.

John Betjeman thought that the only spire that could rival the one at the Triple Kirks was Salisbury Cathedral. For nearly a century and a half it has fitted happily into the Aberdeen skyline. Thirty or forty years ago, the skyline was punctuated by towers and spires — there are some fifty of them in Aberdeen — but the building of skyscraper blocks and other building developments have largely wiped out the impact they once had. In some ways it is sadly symbolic, a sign of the empty pews that lie below many of them.

On the other side of Schoolhill there is a plaque that some people — Gordonians, at anyrate — might regard as a piece of scholastic sacrilege — a Grammar School memorial on a Gordon's College wall. The inscription on it, put up by Aberdeen Grammar School FP's Club in 1930, is a reminder that the Grammar School stood on this site from 1757 to 1863, although it is believed that there was a grammar-school on Schoolhill as far back as the thirteenth century. About a mile away, J. Pittendreigh MacGillivray's statue of Lord Byron stands in front of the modern Grammar School in Carden Place.

Here, Byron has turned his back on his old school, which may be an expression of disapproval at what has been happening to it. Firstly, the town

It was June, 1953, when Aberdeen celebrated the Coronation of the Queen. In little Chestnut Row, the 'dead-end street with live ideas', the residents organised a tea party, a fancy-dress parade for the youngsters, and a picnic — and invited Lord Provost Graham to open the celebrations. Here, the fancy-dress parade is 'piped' off to the picnic in a field where the Norco Superstore now stands.

council turned it into a 'comprehensive' school and stood five centuries of tradition on its head by admitting girl pupils. Then, as if to rub salt in the wound, they stripped it of its name and called it Rubislaw Academy (the High School for Girls became Aberdeen Academy), but such a blast of fury arose from former pupils that in 1977 its old name was restored. The derisive laughter that arose from its old rival, Robert Gordon's College, has now been stilled, for it, too, has opened its doors to girls. The final blow for Grammar came in July, 1986, when it was ravaged by fire. Grampian Regional Council rebuilt it.

Aberdeen has had its share of disasters in the twentieth century. In 1966, another seat of learning not yet in use was devastated when Aberdeen University's partially-built zoology building at Old Aberdeen collapsed. One man was killed and six others trapped when the seven-storey building went down 'like a pack of cards'. Thousands of tons of steel and concrete fell on them and a massive rescue operation got under way. The previous year, 1965, saw the disappearance of the Aberdeen trawler *Blue Crusader*, with a crew of thirteen on board.

The folk of Aberdeen have always thought of themselves as a neighbourly lot, and this was underlined in June 1953 when the city celebrated the

Coronation of the Queen. One small street got special attention from Lord Provost John Graham. He dropped in on an *al fresco* tea party held in Chestnut Row, which became known as 'the dead-end street with live ideas'. The residents organised a fancy-dress parade and a picnic in a field opposite 'The Row'. The Lady Provost, wife of Lord Provost John Graham, opened the celebrations and told the householders that by getting together in such a way and creating neighbourliness they were celebrating the Coronation in the best possible way. 'Three cheers for Chestnut Row!' cried the Lord Provost.

The field in Berryden where the picnic was held is now the site of the Norco Superstore. Back in 1953 it was owned by Northern Marts. Friday was mart day in Aberdeen, the day the country came to town. There was still a Kittybrewster Station then; now both mart and station have gone. The spreading city caught up with the mart, and in the end it became an impossible mix, farmers and cattle dodging traffic on Great Northern Road. There were always newspaper headlines saying, 'Bullock runs amok at Kittybrewster'. The farm hands ate their 'denner' (they call it lunch nowadays) in the Kittybrewster pubs and Mart Luncheon Rooms, but the farmers and their wives dined more elegantly in the Northern Hotel.

The Northern Hotel was one of Aberdeen's leading hotels, for it had the field to itself on the northern rim of the city for many years, but it slipped down the league table as the town spread north and new hotels were built to cater for the growing traffic at Aberdeen Airport. Oil turned a huddle of sheds at Dyce into a jet-age air terminal, and it was at Dyce that Aberdeen officially entered the Oil Age. On November 3, 1975, at BP's Dyce headquarters, the Queen pressed a button which set the whole BP Forties oil system in operation for the first time. A simultaneous electronic signal opened a valve at the Grangemouth gas separation plant and sent the first Forties oil into the refinery. It was the culmination of a £745-million gamble to wrest oil from the North Sea, a build-up that began in October, 1970 when BP disclosed that they had struck oil 110 miles east of Aberdeen.

The Queen said that the story of how North Sea oil was brought ashore was one of excitement and romance. No-one would have argued with that, but a little more than a decade later the Granite City — the Oil City as it had become — discovered that there was a bitter price to pay. In July, 1988, the Piper Alpha

The year was 1983. 'The Dons are the Greatest' said the poster strung across the top of the open-deck bus as it made its way along Union Street. The fans didn't have to be told that they had come out in their thousands to welcome their team home from Gothenburg with the European Cup-Winners Cup. They had won the Scottish Cup that year; now they had brought a European honour to Pittodrie for the first time in the history of Aberdeen F.C. Our picture shows the players and Manager Alex Ferguson on top of their coach as they reached Broad Street, where Lord Provost Alex Collie, a fervent Dons fan himself, was waiting to greet them from the Town House balcony. Out at Pittodrie, 20,000 more fans had turned up to cheer their heroes. Picture by courtesy of' Aberdeen Journals.

rig exploded, a great ball of fire bursting nightmarishly over it. That night, helicopters shuttled backwards and forwards from the scene of the disaster, carrying the dead and the badly-scarred victims of the tragedy to the helicopter pad in the grounds of Aberdeen Royal Infirmary. The toll was 167 dead, with many injured, some severely burned. On top of the physical injuries there were psychological problems to deal with; some survivors would be mentally scarred for life. Many would never set foot on an oil rig again.

In 1989 the official inquiry got under way at Aberdeen Exhibition Centre. The survivors had to re-live their nightmare, describing in long and painful detail what had happened, how they had escaped the inferno by leaping into the blazing sea, swimming for their lives until they were picked up by rescue boats. Some broke down, others hit out at negligence and incompetence. Meanwhile, out at Piper Alpha, the charred remains of the rig stuck up grotesquely above the sea. The dead oilmen's families wanted a halt put on its demolition until a search was carried out for bodies that had not been recovered. Early in April, charges were fixed to the metal spars and the skeleton of the ill-fated rig slipped under the water, out of sight.

The impact of oil on Aberdeen was not always evident to the man-in-the-street. Long after the oil boom was under way the sight of a ten-gallon Stetson still brought a twist of the head from passers-by, but it was more than likely that the wearer was an Aberdeen exile home on holiday from the States. The American oilmen, being an itinerant breed, never knowing how long they would stay in one place, kept themselves to themselves; they had their own school and their own social club. Just how much the Granite City had been affected by oil was best seen in the crowded lounge of Aberdeen Airport, where oil workers waited to board helicopters to fly to the rigs while oil executives jetted up and down to their offices in London. The bigger companies had huge office blocks in Tullos, looking down on a harbour crowded with oil supply ships.

The oil boom brought prosperity, but it also brought rocketing prices. Dining out became an expensive luxury, except for those on expense accounts, and buying a house put the family budget deep into the red. In the summer of 1986 it looked as if the boom had burst; there was a slump in oil prices and the days of the easy 'buck' were over. Some Aberdeen entrepreneurs, sensing what was needed to supply the offshore operations, had made fortunes. There were canny characters like the late Bob Farquhar, whose North-east tongue was as thick as Scotch broth. Behind his broad, homely accent was an astute mind. Bob, who once sold henhouses from a second-hand truck, built portable loos for the oil industry and boasted that he had started his working life 'sellin' sheds, chalets an' shitehooses'.

In time, the oil bubble began to inflate again, and the industry emerged from the slump slimmer and slicker, more prepared for the last decade of the

This was where generations of Aberdonians danced the years away - the Beach Ballroom on the city's seafront. Its octagonal design and high tiled roof won an architectural competition when it was built in 1926, but it has never been a moneyspinner. People didn't want to face the chill sea breezes in midwinter. Now, with the building of an adjoining leisure centre and swimming pool, an ice rink, and a new luxury hotel, life is coming back to the 'Beach'.

century. Back in the early days, the question on most people's lips was 'How long will it last?' The pessimists thought that the oil would dry up before the end of the century, but now the forecasters are looking well beyond the year 2000, to a new boom lasting at least twenty-five years. That the city is firmly established as an international oil centre means that companies will see it as their headquarters for all offshore operations in Europe for a very long time to come. Aberdeen-based companies are already exporting the skills they learned in the North Sea to countries all over the world.

The city's business leaders certainly looked beyond the twentieth century. Working with the public sector, they pondered on such things as city-centre improvements, food technology, tourism, and the commercialisation of academic research. Oil still featured largely in their thinking. The thought of oil as a tourist attraction was an intriguing one, but it went beyond handing out bottles of the black stuff to visitors. The idea was to bring Oil Experience to Aberdeen. The 'Experience' would take the form of a Science and Technology Centre — Scitech — which would feature aspects of the oil industry and life offshore in a way that would be entertaining and informative to family audiences, It would be a combination of 'fun and learning'.' The estimate was that it would attract between 400,000 and 600,000 visitors a year, but as 1998 got under way the Government was urging thrift and purse-strings were tightening.

Aberdonians knew all about thrift, but in the oil-rich years they had learned a few new tricks. The Granite City was geared up for the twenty-first century. What William Robbie said in 1893, writing of a different age, still applied today…that Aberdeen can look back on a century that has seen changes and developments that at one time might have been regarded as extravagant fancies, and that it can look forward knowing that it will stay ahead in the years to come.

Further Reading

Allan, John R. — *The North-east Lowlands of Scotland* (Hale 1952)

Brogden, W.A. — *Aberdeen: an Illustrated Architectural Guide* (Royal Incorporation of Architects in Scotland and Scottish Academic Press 1986)

Buchanan, William — *Glimpses of Olden Days in Aberdeen* (1870)

Carnie, William — *Reporting Reminiscences* (Aberdeen University Press 1902)

Fraser, G. M. — *Aberdeen Street Names* (Bon-Accord Press 1911)

Graham, Cuthbert — *Portrait of Aberdeen and Deeside* (Hale 1972)

Keith, Alexander — *A Thousand Years of Aberdeen* (Aberdeen University Press 1972)

Meldrum, Edward — *Aberdeen of Old* (1986)

Milne, John — *Aberdeen (1911)*

Munro, Alexander M. — *Memorials of the Aldermen, Provosts, and Lord Provosts of Aberdeen* (1897)

Robb, Alexander — *Poems and Songs* (Lewis Smith 1852)

Robbie, William — *Aberdeen: its Traditions and History* (Wyllie 1893)

Rorie, David (Editor) — *The Book of Aberdeen* (British Medical Association 1939)

Skene, William — *East Neuk Chronicles (1905)*

Trail, Katherine E. — *The Story of Old Aberdeen* (Wyllie 1929) and *Reminiscences of Old Aberdeen* (Wyllie 1932)

Wyness, Fenton — *City by the Grey North Sea: Aberdeen* (A.P. Reid 1965)

Index